ON MY WAY
TO
BLUEBIRD
COTTAGE

ISBN 979-8-89309-004-8 (Paperback)
ISBN 979-8-89309-005-5 (Digital)

Covenant Books
11661 Hwy 707
Murrells Inlet, SC 29576
www.covenantbooks.com

ON MY WAY TO BLUEBIRD COTTAGE

by

Joye Frost

COVENANT BOOKS

CONTENTS

DEDICATION

"Jesus, the Author and Finisher of our faith." Hebrews 12:2

INTRODUCTION

Love, Home, and the Heart of Everything

A home can be a shelter from the wind and rain, a place to snuggle up with a great book and hot tea, if that is what you love. It can be a place to store things that you love; things that can never be replaced, such as gifts from the children and their self-portraits, old family photos, and my husband's love letters lovingly tucked away in fancy shoeboxes for a rainy-day browse. I like to think of home, never mind how humble or grand it may be, as a place to feel safe and comfortable but, above all else, where loved ones, at some converging point, come to laugh and hug or even to cry, confiding their deepest mysteries, their own unique selves, despite the pull of mundane everyday life.

There are a great many people, an estimation of over 500,000 in the US alone, as I write this, who are considered to have no home on any given day. I have given this a lot of thought; maybe because home has always meant so much to me. Having moved more times than I could possibly count and having been homeless myself, there were times in which I couldn't see any hope of having the love of family and a place to call home, so I don't take for granted having that refuge in this life.

In those days, I couldn't see how, in this world of pain and struggle, I would end up with a loving family and the love of my life in our own new beautiful home, but here we are. However, there's more to life than having a lovely house. There is joy and peace that nothing in this world can steal away, with the hope of a wonderful new surprise around every corner.

I want you to know that there is always hope and a "tailor-made" future for each one of us, no matter who you are, where you've come from, or what your circumstances may be. Each and every one of us was put here to live an extraordinary life that exceeds the highest expectations, never too early, never too late, especially designed for us, individually unique. We have our hopes and dreams for a reason. My greatest desire has been to find that life and to pass on to you how it all came about.

CHAPTER 1

The Beginning

Working on a Saturday

It's 4:00 a.m., Saturday morning. My alarm goes off, and I fumble to turn it off. I lay there for a moment, then remembered to start my meditation time.

"I am holy." *Deep breath.* "I am in perfect health." *Deep breath.* "I live in a beautiful home that is finished, paid for, and well taken care of. My home is filled with love, creativity, and joy." *Deep breath.* "My family and I are blessed beyond measure." *Deep breath.* "We share our gifts and talents to help and inspire the world."

As I whisper these words into the darkness, I realize that I have a sore throat that feels like I'm swallowing knives. *Must be my sinuses,* I think to myself, but this is worse than usual, and I really don't feel like going to work at all. However, if I give in to that, I'd be ruining my record of never calling in sick or being late in the three years I've worked at my job soldering cables on an assembly line.

I throw the covers off and sit on the side of the bed with thoughts going through my head about wishing I could stay in bed. I feel like crap. It's cold.

I drag myself out of bed and step onto the scale while I wait for the shower water to get hot. "Damn!" Another pound gained. I'm up to 190, and my blood sugar probably reads the same. And after all the dieting and walking I've been doing! *It seems hopeless,* I think to myself, *but I have to get this weight under control, or the doctor will put me back on medication for the diabetes again, in addition to the blood pressure and cholesterol medicine I'm already taking.*

Giving my mostly auburn hair a quick brush, I notice in the mirror that it's time to color the gray again. Downstairs, I'm finally packed and ready for work. I stumble through the dark outside down the driveway, trying not to fall as I trip through the ruts where the rain has washed out the gravel from the driveway again. I juggle coffee, lunch bag, and keys, going down my mental list of things not to forget…hair tie, ID badge, vitamin C drops, safety glasses, mask, phone…lunch…well, that's a given. I'd never forget that.

As I drive out of my driveway at 5:00 a.m., I'm feeling a bit jealous that my husband is still snoring in bed. *He hardly ever has to work on a Saturday!* I grumble to myself. I'm still wiping the sleep from my eyes and take a sip of my coffee as I drive up the winding country road into the cold darkness. The warm liquid feels so good on my throat, though my head is a bit woozy. I didn't have time to read my devotion this morning or say my prayers before heading out. But then there's the long, forty-five-minute drive to work, so that's plenty of time to talk with God, though this morning, feeling like I do, my heart isn't really in it. I'm so stiff and sore that it's an effort to even drive.

"Thank You, Lord, for this beautiful day, for my loved ones, and even my job." I smile at such an ironic prayer and how I'm **"calling things that be not as though they are" (Rom. 4:17)**, at least as far as work is concerned. "Thank You for my husband, the home of my dreams, and my nice new car. And for my coffee!" Saying these words softens my attitude a bit, and I add, "I love You, Lord." I think about what a roller coaster ride life has been even as a child; the riches to rags, the grief and fear, up to the present. I think about all the things that I have now to be grateful for, and I remember the first wish I ever made.

I did not know it as I drove down that dark country road on that early December morning that my life was about to begin a whole new level of blessing. And so, there is no sweeter moment for me than now, as I share my story with you about how every good thing came to pass.

It all started with a prayer, a cardboard box that my mother had lovingly crafted into a dollhouse for me, and my most wonderful counselor and invisible friend whom I named Mrs. Magillacutti.

* * * * *

I heard my great-grandfather, Grampa John, slowly shuffle up the two flights of stairs until he finally reached my little attic room where I waited with great anticipation, dressed in my nightclothes and ready for bed. He stopped at the doorway to catch his breath. He was a heavyset man, mostly bald, but to this five-year-old girl, he was my knight in shining armor, and I was his little princess with big blond curls. He had a magical way of spending the final hour of the day with me and only me.

"Grampa! I have my books picked out!" Every night, he would read three books to me. Tonight, it would be *The Color Kittens* spilling and mixing all their amazing colors together to create a brand-new color; the wonderful adventure in *The Sugarplum Tree*, where there was lots of candy; and the generosity of the elves and good business sense of the shoemaker in *The Shoemaker and the Elves*. Sometimes I imagined the elves sliding down a moonbeam right through my very own bedroom window.

"Well, have you been a good girl for Granny today?" He adjusted his glasses, smiling sweetly and settled down on the edge of the bed to begin our story time.

I tried to think of something good rather than how I had wetted my pants and broken an egg in the backyard. "I dusted for Granny today," I answered humbly.

"Oh, that's quite a job with all the fancy carved furniture she has!" He opened the sweet-smelling pages that held all the wonderful images and secrets of the universe inside; the big new books that Mommy had sent from New York City where she worked as a commercial artist to save up for our new home.

Her picture hung over my bed. She was a classic beauty with dark chestnut-brown hair that framed her heart-shaped face with a perfect "widow's peak" adorning her forehead. Her long, thick braid fell over her shoulder. She wore bright red lipstick.

After story time, Grampa John had me kneel and fold my hands beside the bed to pray. We said it together. "Now I lay me down to sleep. I pray Thee, Lord, Thy child to keep." We never said the usual gruesome stuff like other kids about dying before waking. "God bless Mommy and Granny and Grampa John and everybody. Amen."

"Ah, aren't you forgetting something?" he reminded gently.

"Oh! And guide my little feet up to Thee. Amen."

He gave an approving nod and tucked me in, kissing me on the forehead.

I couldn't read yet, but I had my own little Bible of the Psalms and the New Testament. I knew about God from the Reading Room at the Christian Scientists Church. Every Sunday my great-grandmother, whom I called Granny, would tie two quarters in the corner of my hankie to give at church. Mary Baker Eddy, who started that church, taught "mind over matter." I understood that to mean that we are already healed and protected. That's why I never had to get my immunization shots for school. It didn't really matter, though, because I ended up not going to school after all, but that comes later in the story.

"Now be a good girl and go to sleep." He smiled his wonderful, kind smile. "Your angels are always watching, you know!"

I woke up in my little attic room the next morning sad and lonely. I had been dreaming of Mommy where we had lived in our little house in Florida. In the dream I saw the silhouette of her legs with the sun shining through as I looked up from the floor. We were two happy vagabonds, living off the land. I ran naked in the Florida heat, watching her pull up the blue crab traps from over the side of the bridge, the briny gulf water splashing cool on the pavement in the hot sunshine. The deep blue sky was filled with screeching hungry gulls diving down to get a closer look at our catch. Then we would visit our circle of produce farmers and pick up the wilted vegetables that no one wanted to buy, and Mommy would laugh and talk with them for a while until I got tired and started to cry. The sky would turn bright orange and red as if it were on fire, as the sun began to set. It was time to go home, just us two in our own little paradise.

But all that was over now. As I lay in my little bed, the cold morning came rolling in with waves of tears. As I looked out my window at Lake Eerie, all I could see was a thick blanket of fog. The long, mournful cry of the foghorn resonated with my heavy heart as I wondered what Mommy could be doing now and when I would ever get to see her again. I examined my chubby little fingers and knew I had a long way to go before I could make my own decisions about my life. I sat down on the floor in front of the cardboard dollhouse my mother had lovingly and painstakingly made for me out of boxes and wallpaper with bits of fabric. There weren't any dolls yet, so I imagined the two of us having tea parties in the tidy little kitchen.

"Mommy, I looove our new house! We should invite Mrs. Magillacutti over for tea!" And no sooner had she come to my thoughts than there she was. My wonderful, invisible, although very real friend Mrs. Magillacutti.

"Well, so nice of you to invite me for tea!" I imagined her to be wearing a beautiful light green pouffe dress, elegant yet comfortable for sitting Indian-style to join us. "What a lovely kitchen! Is it everything you wished for?" She leaned forward, pinky extended to smile at me with one raised eyebrow.

I could tell her anything, and she would understand. Now that she was here, the heaviness in my heart was floating away into thin air like the fog lifting from the lake, burned away by the sunshine. "Well, I pray and ask God to someday have a real home and a happy family of my own."

"And what would *you like to do*?" she asked, attentively listening for my answer.

After a bit of thought about how I wanted to be an artist like Mommy, I said, "I would write books that make the whole world happy!" Moving to the round braided multicolored rug on the floor that reminded me of the world, I proceeded to cut tiny pieces from a sheet of white paper like confetti, throwing it up into the air to land all over the rug. They were my books on the four winds, bringing joy to everyone everywhere.

"I wish Mommy were really here," I added, tears welling up again.

"Well, isn't that something!" Mrs. Magillacutti brightly diverted my gloomy thoughts. "If you go downstairs right now, you'll see that she's calling you on the telephone this very minute!"

I raced from my room and bounded down the stairs like a giddy gazelle, disrupting the quiet of the two old people downstairs.

"Granny! Grampa John! Mommy's calling me right now!"

"What on earth…" Granny stammered. "Settle down, now!"

And then, sure enough, the phone rang. It was Mommy.

When they had finished talking, Granny hung up the phone.

I hopped up and down with excitement. "I'm going to visit Mommy in New York City! And she says she has a lot of great surprises to show me!"

"How did you already know Mommy was calling?" Grampa John whispered.

"Mrs. Magillacutti told me," I whispered back.

"Ahhhh." He gave an understanding wink. Granny was the one who went to church to visit God, but Grampa John was the one who knew that the invisible world of angels, good and evil, were everywhere and very real.

After the exciting phone conversation, Granny waved me into my seat at the dining table. "First things first!" She bustled from the kitchen, bringing our breakfast. I had my own boiled egg stand and a ceramic cup that looked like a giraffe with a straw for the neck to drink my juice.

"Sit up straight, and chew with your mouth closed, for heaven's sake!" Granny instructed. She had gone to finishing school as a girl and knew all the manners that a proper lady should know.

"Enough of this dawdling!" Granny tossed her starched white apron aside. "We have a dance recital to attend!" Granny never raised her own daughter, whom I called Nana, but rather had sent her to a private boarding school for girls. It seemed that upon realizing her mistake of not raising Nana, she could now redeem herself by giving me all her attention, trying to teach me all the wisdom she possessed.

Granny shushed me into the bathroom to get ready. "All right! Let's wash up!" she said. "High as possible, low as possible, and don't forget possible!"

Granny was a large woman, but she could really move when she wanted to. The phone call had thrown her schedule off, so she hurriedly dressed me in my pink ballet costume and coat and ushered me to the car. I took my favorite spot, lying up in the back window of the old blue Chrysler, to watch the beautiful maples that lined our street in all their breathtaking splendor of early fall, vivid orange and red against the bright blue sky, as we went whizzing by the lakefront.

The recital was a real success. Afterward, all the dancers were lined up across the stage to take a bow. When the audience finished applauding, the teacher went down the row with the microphone, asking each dancer what they wanted to be when they grew up. I heard "a ballerina," "a nurse," a mommy," and so forth. One little girl said, "A dance teacher," and the audience gave an endearing, "Awwww." I was the last in line as I was the youngest and smallest one in the group.

"And what would you like to be when you grow up, young lady?" she asked, holding the microphone to my face.

I wanted to say something exciting, so I answered proudly, "A damned old witch!"

At first someone gasped. It was silent for a second, then someone started clapping, and everyone roared with laughter.

After the recital, we had refreshments in the front hall, and Granny followed up with the story about how I was kicked out of Catholic school for cursing. "The child is merely expressing herself!" she said.

Granny treated me to my usual hamburger for lunch on the way home from dance. In early fall, it was still warm at noon, so when we got home I was allowed to play in the backyard before it got too cool in the afternoon. I noticed a couple of boys messing around in Granny's rhubarb patch behind the fence. Immediately I ran into the house to alert her. "Are you going to whip their asses, Granny?"

"No, dear. I know who these boys are," she said, grabbing a knife as she looked out the window. "Take my hand, and we'll deal with this a-ppro-pri-ate-ly." She loved using big words and would often break them into syllables to teach them to me. She grabbed my hand, and we hurried out the back door. The boys looked up and started to run. "Wait!" she exclaimed. "You boys can have all you want!" she called.

They stopped and froze with surprised looks on their faces. "Sorry, ma'am. We were taking some for our mom to make a pie." They were wearing old clothes and had dirty faces. I wondered why. *Maybe they're poor*, I thought.

"Well, you'll need more than that," Granny answered. "But you need to be a good neighbor and ask before you take it next time. If you'll do that, then I might have some odd jobs that you could do to earn a little extra money." Granny cut a generous amount and handed them each a bundle.

The boys shot an excited glance at one another and gave a hearty "thank you" as they took off with their prize.

"Aren't you mad 'cause they were stealing your rhubarb, Granny?" I asked as we walked back to the house.

"If I got mad and chased them, they would just come back again when I wasn't looking and steal some more, but this way I can help them to understand what it is to be a good neighbor. One thing you must always remember, Joye, love reflects love. Besides, I need the fence painted, and your Grampa certainly isn't going to do it!" She chuckled.

That afternoon, Grampa John and I sat on the front screened porch, smelling the fresh-cut grass and gazing out at the lake, he from his rocker and I from my own little white wicker chair. Grampa John was very tired. We were silently waiting with excited anticipation, watching for Mommy to arrive.

"Here you go, Sweet Pea." He handed me my own little mug of beer that matched his big mug of beer.

"There's a damned old spider, Grampa!" I pointed my chubby finger at the corner of the porch.

"Well, kick 'em in the ass and kill 'em!" he replied.

I got up, eager to comply. "Bastard!" I exclaimed, heartily stomping the culprit underfoot.

It was 1964. Mommy took me to visit her for two weeks. We arrived at night, with my face pressed to the window of the cab to see the spectacle of lights that shone before us. As we crossed the George Washington Bridge, Mommy held me close and pointed to the lights. "Look, honey, it's just like a fairyland!" It was the most amazing entrance to the city, more beautiful than I could ever have imagined.

When we arrived at her apartment in Manhattan, Mommy gave the cabdriver a fistful of cash, and he left us standing there on the dirty sidewalk. There were people out, everywhere, even at night. The city close-up was dirty and smelly. It was almost like Mommy read my thoughts and took a long, deep breath, inhaling through her nose. "You smell that?" She let her breath out with a burst. "It's garbage!" she exclaimed proudly, laughing her lust-for-life laugh.

When I walked into her apartment, the first thing to catch my eye were two huge red-and-gold dragon masks from the Chinese New Year parade; they hung in two opposite corners of her one-room flat.

Two big all-black Persian-Angora cats sauntered up to greet us. "Meet my roommates, Joye! Damien! Pithius!" Mommy said, rubbing them on the sides of their black furry heads. "Did you miss me?" They returned her rubbing and rubbed on me too. Suddenly a voice from the kitchen cried out, "Key wow wow!" Mommy took me by the hand and led me to the kitchen. "And this is my friend the mynah bird, Murry Shwartz. I found him on the roof with the pigeons, and he just decided to come on in and live with us too!"

Mommy made us a quick snack. I fed Murry some of my canned mixed fruit from the end of a chopstick so he wouldn't bite my fingers off. We ate bagels and lox before bed. Everything was different, like being in another world.

In the morning, Mommy got dressed while I watched Felix the Cat and Astro Boy cartoons on TV for the first time. Then Mommy took me downstairs to the sidewalk. There were so many people! "Climb in." She held a shopping cart for me while I scampered into it, and away we went. "We have a busy day so we're going for the best breakfast Manhattan has to offer!" She stopped by the hot dog stand to get us each a hot dog with mustard and then, of course, Mommy's favorite, the coffee shop.

When we arrived at the World's Fair, the overwhelming smell of cotton candy took over right inside the gate. The air was electric, and I felt like my heart would burst with excitement. Everywhere I looked, something marvelous was happening. There were rides that looked like rockets zooming around planets, whirling and dipping with people laughing and screaming.

"Where will we go first?" I pulled on her sleeve anxiously.

Mommy took me on all the rides. We could see the whole park from the elevated monorail train. We saw the exhibit of the first home computers that would soon be available to the public. We saw the debut of *Mary Poppins*, larger than life on the big screen. What a wonderful day it was!

When we got back to Manhattan, I went back into the shopping cart, and we headed for Mommy's Asian shop-owner friend Margarite's for a nighttime snack.

"Hello!" Margarite greeted us with her beautiful smile. "So this is our little princess that your Mommy told me so much about!" she said with her funny accent. The air was thick with the smell of strange spices.

She gave me one of the paper-wrapped balls with a toy surprise in the middle, the kind that Mommy had sent to me in the mail at Granny's, and a snack of salty fish on a string. There were rows and rows of so many things I had never seen before. Mommy told me to pick a toy, and I chose a wiggly snake made of wooden parts all held together by metal links.

That week, we took an elevator to the top of the Empire State Building, where I discovered that I was terrified of heights and have been ever since.

We climbed the Statue of Liberty. We couldn't go into the arm because it was under repair. From the crown, we could see the whole city. I was afraid, but Mommy knelt down and held me close to her side. She softly spoke to me, saying, "Isn't it a beautiful world? I'm taking you back to Granny's tomorrow, but don't forget that I am working very hard to pay for a special home that was custom-designed for you and me. We will have this wonderful home moved to sunny Florida very soon, and there we will live, happily ever after."

I forgot all about Mrs. Magillacutti during this time of excitement and bliss.

When I returned to the house in Canada, the house was empty, the car was packed, and Granny climbed into the passenger's side of her old blue Chrysler, mopping her weepy eyes.

Nana was in the driver's seat and about to back out of the driveway. She was dressed nicely with her hair in a braided bun on top of her head, her wispy brown strands hair-sprayed into place.

When I inquired, "Where's Grampa John?" Granny and Nana exchanged looks. Nana answered with seemingly little emotion, "He's gone on the Big Vacation."

"In heaven," Granny added through tears. I understood that meant he passed away. A "Big Vacation" made it seem like we would see each other again and made me not feel so sad. Nana proceeded to back out of the driveway. We were off to sunny Florida, but farther away from Mommy.

CHAPTER 2

Survival Mode

Home with Nana and Grampa in St. Petersburg, FL

Mom was still working in New York City, so when I was seven, I was sent to stay with her mom and dad, whom I called Nana and Grampa Calvert. They lived in St. Pete, Florida, and they didn't seem very happy with the idea of taking me in.

They didn't send me to school, but I got to stay outside and play all day.

Grampa spied my handiwork of broken banana branches and holes in the yard as he came stomping and cursing out the back door. "You damn little devil! Look what you've done!"

It was Florida summer heat, and we had no AC in those days. I had been breaking the banana tree branches in the heavy dew of early morning to catch the little green tree frogs before the day became a sweltering 100 degrees. Now I was ambitiously digging holes in the yard that would catch the afternoon thundershowers, creating my own swimming pool. I dropped the shovel and ran away from Grampa, who chased me hysterically with the rake. The veins popping out on his forehead and his blood-red face was scary, for sure, but I couldn't help myself from laughing. I knew he couldn't catch me and thought to do what I usually did—hide in the woods until almost dark. By then, he would have cooled down and it would be safe to come back. But then Nana unexpectedly appeared on the scene. She wasn't anything like Granny, and Grampa Calvert wasn't anything like Grampa John. Nana was dark brown from the sun, with wispy brown hair that flew in every direction. She was fast as a whip and didn't play around. There was nothing that she couldn't do.

"Come here!" Nana called. I knew I had better come too, because if *she* caught me, she would be giving my legs a good switching. Nana grabbed my arm, pulling me down with a hard plop on the back concrete steps. She yanked my matted, dirty blond hair with a brush and whacked me with it when I shrieked and tried to get away. She found a tick on me, pulled it off, and burned it to death next to my leg, on the concrete steps, with her cigarette. The three of us got into the car.

Grampa drove us to the strip mall where the grocery store was, past the A&W, turned right to the big highway, turned in front of the big pink house with the pretty garden, past the gas station, past the drugstore… "What Comes Next" was a game I played with myself to remember the way home.

Nana directed me to a coin-operated horse to ride. I sat on it and pretended to ride. "Now you stay there until we get finished with our shopping," she instructed, and they disappeared. Grampa shuffled off pushing the cart around the corner and into the store.

I knew it was up to me to figure out how to get home when the sun started going down and they didn't come back for me. I started walking and found my way back home, but "home before dark" was the rule, so I knew I'd get a good switching if I got caught coming in that late. I snuck quietly in the back kitchen door, quickly slipping under the dining table to hide beneath the tablecloth. The dinner plates hadn't been cleared yet. I watched Nana's legs move hurriedly about the kitchen to fix a fresh pot of coffee. She left the kitchen. Now was my chance. After a fast scan of the top of the table, I grabbed what I saw. There weren't any leftovers on their plates, so I quickly returned to my hiding place, with a soft stick of butter in the butter dish and a cup of leftover black coffee to wash it down with. I didn't mind such a weird supper. I absolutely *loved* butter *and* coffee, and at least I didn't have to choke down Nana's instant mashed potatoes. Then I hid behind the end of the couch and peeked over the dark greasy arm to watch the end of *Flipper* and *20,000 Leagues Under the Sea*. Sleep was taking over by then, so I ever so quietly slipped off to bed in the spare bedroom that used to be Aunt Martha's.

I woke up in the middle of the night with a terrible bellyache. I walked to the living room holding my stomach and crying.

Nana came stomping out of the bedroom. "Shhhh!" she implored with a loud whisper. "You'll wake your grandfather!"

"I have a bellyache!" I cried.

Nana sat in the rockless rocker and motioned me over. "Have you been in that damn crabapple tree again? What did I tell you about that?"

"I only ate a few!" I climbed up in her lap. I had forgotten to take my shoes off before I went to bed. The little red sneakers that Granny and Grampa John had bought me had holes in both of the toes now. Nana smoothed the frays down on the holes and sang me a little song in her deeper voice, the one for making me go to sleep, while she rocked. Her deep tone as I laid my head on her chest *was* soothing. She sang,

> Oh, the rich gal wears the ruffles on her drawers,
> The poor gal wears 'em plain.
> The other gal don't wear no drawers at all,
> but she gets there just the same.
> Well, it ain't gonna rain no more, no more.
> It ain't gonna rain no more.

Home with Mommy at Park Lane Trailer Park, FL

I didn't stay with Nana and Grampa for very long. Mommy came for me one day, and we got to move together to Pinellas Park, Florida, to a place called Park Lane Trailer Park. Our new home was a beautiful long white mobile home called the "Kroft" with wood paneling all through the inside that I loved to imagine had strange tree faces in the wood grain. I had my own little room with built-in bunks, cubbies at the foot, and a little window at the side to look out of and see the stars at night. It had big closets and a built-in desk. Mommy and I finally had our little dream castle together.

Mommy built a beautiful fishpond at the front of the trailer. She planted big elephant ear plants around the pond—which hid the hitch, she said—and placed a green concrete frog that joyfully spit water into the pond filled with big fat goldfish. We had a lovely patio at the side made of steppingstones that was surrounded by bottlebrush trees with their peeling paper-like bark and odd-smelling red flowers that really looked just like bottlebrushes!

Mommy was amazing. She owned her own art store full of every kind of art supply. It was called Florida Art and Photo in St. Petersburg. I spent many nights sleeping on a cot there in the back while she worked taking passport photos and retouching photos and other orders for photo coloring that came in. For lunch, I could walk down the street to the White Castle to get us burgers and play "Wendy" on the jukebox while I waited. Of course, if there was an old doll in the window of the Goodwill that I passed on the way, I would have to "adopt" her with the change I had left over from our burgers. Mommy and I would make her something pretty to wear out of napkins and tape.

I didn't go to school then either, so when we were home, I was free to roam and ride my bike up and down the drive between the long rows of mobile homes.

It was wonderful. My long blond curls and sparkly pink plastic bike handle pom-poms blew in the warm Florida breeze as I flew along the road on my bike between the long rows of trailers. I was wearing my pretty new sundress, white with big yellow flowers.

"Little girl!" a neighbor called from his screen porch. He was an elderly man who lived down the way, a little heavyset with white hair. "I have a lot of candy here left over from my granddaughter's party. Would you like some to take home?"

How exciting! Free candy! I thought. "Sure!"

Mommy had told me not to throw my bike down and scratch it up, so I carefully put the kickstand down and entered the screen porch. He sat on a sofa next to an end table that had a bowl of different types of candy.

"Come sit over here by me," he said, motioning. After handing me a piece of candy, he pulled me close and reached for a jar of Vaseline.

New Jersey

Despite my embarrassment, I told Mom what happened, and she told me not to go back over there, which I certainly had no desire to do anyway. I was deeply ashamed and a bit bewildered too.

I couldn't help but wonder, did this happen to all girls? Or was it just something about me that made it happen to me? Was it something I did? Should I have known better?

Even though I had a lot of questions, I didn't want to talk about it. I felt stupid and weird and gross because I was afraid to say no and run away from that neighbor like I should have.

I was eight when the "neighbor incident" happened, then Mom got cancer. Her cancer changed everything. My brother, Bryan, had just been born, so we packed a small U-Haul, with the dog, the cat, and the fish on the back seat of our Volkswagen bug. I lay on the floor with my legs over the hump. Mom was nursing my baby brother while she drove from St. Pete, Florida, to Matawan, New Jersey. His bassinette was in the passenger's seat.

Mom bravely fought cancer five times during her life. I don't ever remember her ever being angry or complaining or feeling sorry for herself. The first time she got sick, we were moving to New Jersey to be near my brother's father in New York so she could work on the freelance work that he provided on his occasional visits. The work was touching up pornography photos, which would make some fast cash needed for her upcoming surgery. We had a small upstairs apartment in the "projects," and her work area was set up in the dining area. There was a slanted table with a light and piles of photos that were stacked higher than I was tall, to touch up naked or near-naked women in all sorts of poses.

He was a cartoonist, and one shocking scenario was a cartoon of a woman being hung by her pubic hair. Mom lettered in the scripts for all the cartoons.

I remember rarely, if ever, going to school up to this point in my life. While Mom slept, I took care of myself and my brother. I avoided school, anyway, because the few times I remember going, no one liked me. In fact, they hated me.

My mother had dropped me off there about an hour late, interrupting class. My teacher, Mr. Thomas, stopped in midsentence as I entered the classroom, then said, "Well, look who decided to show up!"

Some kids snickered as I found my empty seat. There was a worksheet waiting for me on the desk, but I had to ask for a pencil. I could read the instructions at the top of the paper, but I didn't understand what they meant. It was a map of the United States with the names of the states down the side of the page. *This is pretty easy,* I thought, quickly making up my own rules. *I'll just draw a line from the state names to all the states I know.* Then I noticed a map on the wall and started drawing lines like crazy. *Let's see... Florida, New York, New Jersey...*

"Okay, times up!" barked Mr. Thomas. He was a slim man with dark hair wearing black-rimmed glasses and a stern look mixed with sarcasm on his face. "Fold your paper 'hot dog' and pass them up to the front."

Hot dog? I had no idea that meant lengthwise and proceeded to fold mine "hamburger" and pass it forward.

"Joye!" He curled a bony finger, looking over his black-rimmed glasses, to motion me to his desk. I rose and reluctantly walked forward. "Are you deliberately doing the opposite of my instructions or are you just stupid?" He refolded the paper in question and opened it abruptly.

More snickering broke out across the room.

"What's more, you cheated!"

I couldn't imagine what he meant unless he considered leaving the answers for the whole class in plain sight "cheating," and to my surprise, I saw that it was even someone else's paper with no name at the top of the paper! But when I meekly tried to explain, he marked a big red "0" at the top and sent me back to my seat. On the way back down the aisle, some girls on the next row were making horrible faces at me.

"Oh my god! It's stinky girl!" one said.

Another whispered loudly, "Pissy pants!"

"Disgusting!" said another. "She must be retarded!"

They all held their noses and scooted in their desks away from me. No wonder. I didn't like taking baths, I wet the bed most nights, and we didn't have a washer in our apartment.

A nervous, ugly little font started to form at the back of my mind...*stupid, cheater, stinky, pissy, disgusting, retarded...little devil.* The words wound around and around in my mind, trying to wiggle down into my heart, into my very being.

And so it went with school, and that's why I took care of my brother and never tried to wake Mom to take me back again. She usually worked all night while we slept, and it was my job to help out in the daytime. "All for one and one for all!" she would say. "Like the Three Musketeers."

Mom never did dishes. She had so many sets of dirty dishes that they were stacked like little towers all over the counters and table. It was my job to do "one dishpan full" a day. Usually, I just filled up the dishpan and let them soak while I played in the bubbles, then put them into the drain rack to dry. The trick was to find the ones that didn't have cigarettes put out in them. Unfortunately, this is how I learned that leaving soap on the dishes can cause diarrhea.

I would go off and leave Bryan playing there. His crying never woke Mom up. I'd head to the store to find something to eat. There was a store down the street, and it was easy to walk in beside a grown-up and fill my pants with candy or whatever I wanted when no one was looking.

I'd say I was an expert thief by the age of nine, but my code of ethics was that I didn't steal from people I knew, just stores. They could afford it. It became a real habit since it was so easy to get away with.

When Bryan's dad came to visit, I had to "take the baby out for a walk" in the stroller. There was a playground, if you could call it that, just across the street from our apartment. It was all dirt with all the swings broken and a dilapidated chain-link fence. One summer, someone fixed the slide, so I went to try it out and burned the backside of my legs.

Once in the winter, I took Bryan to skate on the ice, but we fell through and got soaking wet. It was freezing, and we couldn't get back into the apartment, so I took him down to the basement where the coin laundry room was. Luckily, the dryer was going with somebody's clothes, so I took the warm clothes from the dryer to dress us. We laughed about the gloves making us look like we had monkey feet.

Before long, I was considered truant, and Mom sent me to live with Nana and Grampa again.

Home with Nana and Grampa in North Carolina

Although I was nine, Mom told the flight attendant that I was twelve, so they let me and my brother fly unaccompanied by an adult. When Bryan and I arrived in North Carolina, Nana drove us to Granny's rented house. It was a little cottage of stone and wood siding painted a cheerful yellow, tucked in among giant hemlock trees deep in the woods at the foot of Mount Pisgah. It was magical. I had never experienced so much beauty in one place before in my life. The air was sweet with the smell of honeysuckle, and good things to eat were everywhere. There was a cool, shallow creek behind the house filled with flecks of glistening gold mica and little crayfish hiding beneath the smooth, moss-covered rocks. A large, thick patch of deep-purple irises grew by the old stone chimney at the side of the house, and apple trees dotted the backyard. Big bunches of dark-purple muscadine grapes hung heavy over the rusty old swing set. A swing set that wasn't broken! Swing "squeeeek"…pick a grape to pop into my mouth…swing "squeeeeek"…pick a grape to pop into my mouth…so very sweet and juicy! I could do this all day! There were wild strawberries growing all over the yard, and huge chestnut trees dropped their delectable soft-shell nuts up and down the dirt roadway.

Bryan ended up staying there at Chestnut Creek with Granny, and I went to stay with Nana and Grampa on Warren Creek, a few miles away, on a forty-plus-acre farm way up in a cove, which they had bought from a friend they'd met in Florida. This was a welcome relief since I would no longer be responsible for the care and safety, if you could call it that, of my little brother. And Granny was crazy about him.

I was nine now and old enough to get myself up, take a shower, and be ready on time for the school bus that stopped right at our front yard every morning. The kids and my fifth grade teacher, Mrs. Coats, were friendly, so I did very well to catch up quickly. I spent every free hour after school and on weekends out of my grandfather's hair, building forts up in the woods and playing in the big creek that cheerfully wound down the length of their property, which spanned two mountainsides in the Great Smokies. They were the happiest days of my life. There was a whole mountainside of huge raspberries to eat, not to mention three big gardens full of every vegetable you can imagine. It was my job to help out with feeding the chickens and planting and weeding the gardens when I got home from school.

Nana's rule was "Hurry up with the chores so we can do something fun!"

Nana had just one speed when she drove, and that was pedal-to-the-floor. We screeched around the sharp curves in her old light-blue Mercury all the way up Mount Pisgah to pick as many buckets of wild blueberries as we wanted. I was good company for Nana. "Now watch for snakes!" she warned. Nana was terrified of snakes, and I wasn't. I was proud to be kind of a lookout and her personal bodyguard. Driving home, ashes flew in the wind from her lit cigarette hanging from a corner of her mouth, around our heads and out the open car windows.

We got home at dinnertime.

"Putt!" Nana called Grampa, sleeping in his chair. "Look what we got for the freezer!" Nana proudly hugged me sideways after we set all our prize pickings before him. Nana's pride and that sideways hug made me feel like I really belonged. "Hot dogs for dinner tonight!" she proclaimed. *Easy and greasy*, I thought. But that was okay. It tasted a lot better than the greasier ducks she cooked from time to time.

After dinner, I got paid for a week of washing the dishes. "Here's your fifty cents, Joye." I hid it in my room, but somehow, she always found it and took it back. It was all right, though. I didn't need money, really.

Nana could make anything. In the evenings, she taught me how to crochet, macramé, and sew. She was an excellent seamstress and made all my clothes for school, of which I was very proud of. When Aunt Martha was starting her career as a dancer, Nana made all her elaborate costumes, sewing on every bugle bead by hand. Aunt Martha then traveled the world dancing in a troupe through Europe and the Middle East.

We had only one TV channel in the mountains, and usually Grampa watched the TV, but tonight there was a special program on. I got cozy with a can of black olives as a special treat to watch Billy Graham's *Crusade* for the first time. The camera panned to show the vast crowd. I had never seen so many people all in one place!

He began, "Tonight, I am speaking primarily to the young people."

Oh, that's me! I thought.

"Now in the fifth chapter of Acts and verse 6. Just one phrase I am going to take completely out of context. 'And the young man arose.'"

I didn't have a Bible to see what "out of context" meant, but I listened intently to his sermon.

"Young people, arise! Go forth to change the world! Begin to march for Jesus Christ!" he proclaimed in a powerful voice. "Young people and every generation have been deceived. The devil's lie is 'give your life to pleasure, to money, to drugs for peace of mind.' But soon you'll find yourselves in bondage. People are being brainwashed every day. I fear even the church will deceive you from the real Jesus. But the real Christ forgives and satisfies and changes and transforms and will hold your hand and be your friend." He went on to talk about how materialism and glamour doesn't satisfy. He talked about sin and how Jesus is the only cure. He spoke about the challenge to follow Christ and how the Holy Spirit gives us power to overcome. He urged everyone to come forward publicly and say yes to Christ.

Well, I thought to myself, *my life isn't so bad, and I haven't even begun to really live my life yet! I want to have fun! There're so many adventures I haven't experienced! I can't just live the rest of my life like a nun!*

That night, I had a dream that Jesus was showing me, on what looked like a big movie screen, about the martyrs who gave their lives for their profession of faith in Christ in the Roman arenas with the lions. The memory of this dream made such an impression on me that it has stayed with me all my life. I remember wondering why anyone would give their lives to do such a thing as getting eaten by a lion.

And so, I didn't fully understand the scope of the decision I had just made, but I had indeed rejected Christ's calling at thirteen years old.

CHAPTER 3

The Downward Spiral of Self-Destruction

Terrible Teen

Granny was in her eighties now. Mom had moved into the little house on Chestnut Creek, and Granny was renting the old farmhouse a few miles down the road from Nana and Grampa's farm.

Nana turned to me at dinner. "Joye, we've decided that it would be best if you went to stay with Granny since she needs help with the housework and she's getting sick a lot more often these days. Pack up your things tonight, and I'll take you down to her house."

My heart sank. This decision made me very unhappy and very angry, though my pride wouldn't let me show it. Had I done something wrong for them to want to send me away again? I wondered. My life of happily roaming the mountainside would be over now. Now I would be taking care of Granny *and* my brother again!

I had worked hard to help Nana all summer, and now that we had everything "put up" in canning jars or the freezer, she was sending me away.

"I'm going up to my fort," I announced as I headed out the door. Nana put the dinner dishes into the sink. This would be my last night with Nana and Grampa.

She nodded.

I had new ugly words swimming around in the back of my mind as I headed up the mountain. *They're throwing you away again…like trash.*

I trekked up the old logging road past Uncle Paul and Aunt Brenda's trailer on the hillside. Aunt Brenda was a small, pretty woman who the family shunned because she had married Uncle Paul so young. She was only six years older than me. I almost always stopped by to see her on my way up to my fort, but today I wasn't in the mood to visit or say goodbye. I was angry about having to leave. I could hear her from the road as I passed by. With her being so petite, it was funny to listen to her heavy footsteps as she walked through the mobile home, from one end to the other. *I guess our days of playing Rummy are over too*, I thought. *What a shame*, I fumed. *We had so much fun together.*

The old dirt logging road was washed out past Paul and Brenda's trailer. I had planned to keep going up past my fort, but first I wanted to stop and check it out to see if there was any storm damage. The lookout platform up in the tree looked fine, so I followed my dugout spiral staircase made of flat stones down around the base of the tree to the room I had dug out under the roots at the side of the bank. I'd made a sort of pergola-type roof out of sticks, but a few had fallen in. *Oh well, who cares? I won't be here tomorrow anyway.*

I followed the little creek up to the springhead. I folded a laurel leaf to make a cup to drink the cool, sweet, refreshing water. A limb had fallen off beside one of the large oaks. I picked it up and started beating the tree with it as hard as I could. That was when the tears began to flow. I took a deep breath and screamed as loud as I could. The birds flew off in a panic. My screams echoed across the mountainside and returned to me with an emptiness in the quiet woods.

Despite my protests later that evening, I sadly said goodbye to Nana's nightly "craft classes," the farm's lush gardens, my beloved forts throughout the woods, and the creek's cool water to wade in up Warren Creek Road.

Granny had turned over the house on Chestnut Creek Road to Mom, but Mom was sick again and wasn't working, so Granny covered her rent.

Granny had rented an old farmhouse just a mile or two down the road from Nana and Grampa. Nana drove me there, while I stared down at the big black garbage bag that held my stuff in my lap. *Just like worthless garbage*, rang through my mind, over and over.

At this point, my life began to take a turn for the worst.

I stayed sad and depressed and didn't really know why. Life seemed so looming and hopeless. Looking ahead, I feared high school and couldn't see myself going on to school or succeeding at any worthy endeavor. I took a handful of Granny's pills, hoping to never have to wake up again, but they just made me really sick. I had chills and threw up all day the next day.

Granny made me go to the little Methodist church down the road once in a while, when she was feeling up to it, but I found it boring, except for the occasional potluck Sundays where I would load up on three heaping plates of food. Those old ladies could really cook!

I retreated into my own little world under a black light in the closet. I lay there in a little bed that I had fashioned out of old blankets, just staring at the wall night after night, listening to Black Sabbath and Alice Cooper records, feeling more and more depressed.

My chores were done at bare minimum and with a terrible attitude. I thought it was funny to mock Granny's shuffle-walk and just ignored my brother.

It was the end of the eighth grade, so I still got myself up and ready to catch the school bus that went right by Granny's house every morning. I met a boy on the bus and started sneaking out my window at night to meet him at the barn behind the house just for something exciting to do. He stopped meeting me, though, when I told him I didn't want to have sex. The last thing I needed right now was to get pregnant. Besides, after raising my brother, I *never* wanted to have kids anyway.

It was another boring weekend.

Every morning, Granny would have toast and coffee and play two games of solitaire. Then Nana and Mom would join her to have coffee around the kitchen table and discuss whatever came to mind.

To hang around and listen to their conversations was a favorite pastime of mine when I was home from school on the weekends.

Granny and I sat at the kitchen table as she paused from her morning game of solitaire to listen over the belting out of "Nothin' could be finer than to be in Carolina in the mooooornin'" on the WWNC radio. Oh, how I hated that whiney country music! I was so amazed how she could listen to that stuff, being an accomplished pianist of classical music. Thankfully, she turned the radio off as we listened to the familiar loud revving of the old light-blue Ford Mercury at the bottom of the driveway.

"Your Nana's here," Granny announced, glancing my way.

Nana came spinning gravel into a cloud of dust as she came barreling up the twists and turns of the steep driveway to Granny's house up on the hill. It was an old white two-story wooden farmhouse that she had rented for a good price from the old man across the street. I found it to be a creepy old house, built back in the days when they only had a saw and a hammer. It had a very narrow stairway that led up to a dusty, musty attic and a multitude of flies gathering on the outside walls in spring.

There was a reason I looked forward to listening in on those morning conversations around the table on the weekends. It was a ritual of chain-smoking, pouring and sipping coffee, and telling wild tales of days gone by, but unfortunately, today the conversation would turn out to be about something different.

Looking out the kitchen window, I saw Nana slam the car door. Her already dark complexion was well browned by the sun. She switched her wide hips, clad in men's old plaid shorts, carrying eggs and potatoes from the farm for Granny and Mom. Her eggs, potatoes, and Mom's government cheese fed me during my four years of high school.

Nana came in like a whirlwind, letting the screen door slam behind her, ashes flying from the Newport cigarette that hung from the corner of her mouth. Granny tried to yell, "Don't slam the…" but Nana cut her off with, "Did you beat Ol' Sol this morning?" She was referring to Granny's morning ritual of three games of solitaire. Nana's wispy brown hair flew in every direction as she wiped her nose down her sleeve and placed the eggs in the refrigerator. She poured herself a cup of hot dark coffee, adding a splash of cream.

Nana took a deep draw from her cigarette and plunked down on a chair at the table, vigorously scratching an ear canal with her pinkie finger. Granny struck a match and lit herself a Belair cigarette as well. Surprisingly, she had taken up smoking a corncob pipe at night also, maybe to embrace this country setting that she had grown so fond of. That meant I had Swisher Sweet tobacco to enjoy on my retreats to the old tobacco barn, in addition to my girlfriend's weed that had grown taller than her house rooftop, conveniently up the road. We liked to roll it up in its own leaves and smoke it like cigars.

Granny sat erect and placid at the head of the table, gently sipping her coffee from one of her matching china tea sets, always the refined lady, yet she kept her gray hair cut short like a man's. "Oh, yes, I did beat Ol' Sol. He keeps me sharp as a tack! Thank you for the eggs, Margaretta. I was planning to make a brown Betty, but it may have to be a custard now." She showed her satisfaction with a pucker of her lips to conceal a slight smile. Granny was an excellent cook.

Last but not least, my mother arrived, driving up slowly in her old blue station wagon "packed to the gills," as Granny often said. She sat out in the car for a good while before her red-bandana-covered head emerged. She had a Lark cigarette already lit and her large yellow "smile" coffee mug in hand.

When she entered the kitchen, Nana was looking inquisitively out the window.

"For Christ's sake, Mary Jane! What the hell is that piled up in the back of the car now?" Nana wondered, loudly.

I already knew. Mom had picked me up for a change on Friday from detention after school, much to my dismay and embarrassment, with the back of the station wagon packed to the top with crates of live chickens. But that wasn't nearly as bad as the time she camped on the side of the highway under tar paper next to an overturned trailer that she intended to salvage, crowbar in hand, waiting to whack anyone trying to muscle in on her claim. No, that outdid the chickens by far. Uncle Paul finally had to roll up the "rescued" carpet for her and bring it home in the back of his truck before she would listen to reason and come home. It was a small town, so everyone knew about it. Everyone called her "the crazy lady." We got funny looks everywhere we went. I felt like trash. Ugly words in my mind said over and over, *you should be ashamed.* And I was.

"Well, I couldn't very well leave them for the raccoons to eat, poor things!" Mom answered out of breath. She was always rescuing something, but it seemed to me that she was the one that needed rescuing. She collected and hoarded animals, trash…everything. She had lost so much after all, she once reasoned in one of our all-night conversations.

Nana raised an eyebrow and twisted the corner of her mouth disgustedly, but we all knew it wouldn't do any good to try and change Mom. She always had her own agenda that no one ever understood, from packing every available living space from floor to ceiling with anything she could find or anything that she felt needed a home, to staying awake for days on end and sleeping for weeks on end. It was all overwhelming and angered me to no end, but I just tried to ignore it as much as possible. We had to walk sideways through narrow trails of floor-to-ceiling boxes through her house when we visited. Bryan had found an old dog he named Fido, and no one ever actually knew how many cats she had. All the animals were sick. Mom was sick. *Life is a sad and overwhelming tragedy* was the dirge that played in the back of my mind whenever I went over to Mom's. I couldn't wait to leave.

The three of them sat at the table with their coffee and cigarettes. The smoke was getting thick in the small kitchen, so I started to get up and go sneak a smoke outside by myself, but Granny caught me. "What's that commercial we watch on TV, Joye?"

I knew which one she was referring to, but I felt stupid reciting it again for her. "Oh, I don't know," I answered, annoyed, rising from my chair.

"Tell it to your mother," Granny persisted.

I thought, *Just get it over and done with*, so I quoted, "Spain! Greece! London! France! I've traveled all over the world…" I didn't realize it at the time, but she was getting us kids to practice faith.

Calling those things that are not as though they were. (Rom. 4:11)

Granny always held Bryan in her lap and asked him, "Who's the smartest boy in town?" and made him recite, "I'm the smartest boy in town, Granny!" In her way, she wanted us to live good lives, travel, and go to college; to be happy and successful. Unfortunately, those were the furthest things from my mind at that time, and I had no clue as to how I would ever accomplish any of that. For me, life was all about having fun and trying everything at least once. And, at thirteen, that was what I had already decided to do.

"Yes, but that's not going to happen when you're sneaking out the window to meet boys at night," Granny added cooly, tapping her cigarette in the ashtray.

"Your grandmother doesn't have the strength to deal with your shenanigans," added Nana. "Pack up your things so you can ride home with your mother."

Mom just looked down at the table and sighed. I guess she was ashamed of me too.

What I didn't expect that day was being told to get my things and leave. Again.

Drunk and High School

Granny sent me and my brother to Mom's. I started high school that fall.

Our magical cottage in the woods on Chestnut Creek had turned into a freezer that winter. I had passed out in my clothes and coat that smelled like woodsmoke and liquor from the previous night's bonfire up on the mountain with my friends. The windup alarm sounded. It was time to get up for school. I started up my record player with Deep Purple to start my day. It was loud, but I didn't care. Mom had been sleeping for weeks now anyway. I didn't bother waking Bryan. That would just be a fight.

The winter's freezing temperatures had left us with broken pipes and no running water, so I grabbed the flashlight and walked out to the reservoir just past the creek in the woods to get a bucket of water to wash myself with. The cold water stung the blisters on my hands from chopping wood for the fireplace, but there was no time to build a fire right now. Scooting sideways through ceiling-to-floor boxes, trying not to slosh the bucket, and clearing a spot on the gas stove, I heated the water. As always, there were piles of dirty dishes everywhere, but in addition to that were the petrifying remains of maggot-eaten tomatoes covering the kitchen table and the overpowering smell of cat poop. Mom made jokes about throwing wood chips down on the floor instead of mopping. Floor? Not funny, in my opinion. Nana had brought us eggs, and we had a giant block of government cheese. In a small skillet I had wiped out and hidden for myself, I quickly made an omelet, then got ready for school.

My best friend, Colin, lived at the beginning of our road. I had been catching a ride with him to school. We did stuff together all the time like go to the movies or just ride around. He totally accepted Mom.

He answered the door. "Hey, hang on! I'll grab my stuff!" I waited outside on the back steps while he grabbed his book bag and kissed his mother goodbye. Warm air wafted out from inside the open door. Their house was neat as a pin.

"I love you! Have a good day!" she called as we rushed off to get into his white Plymouth Duster.

"Love you too, Mom!"

"Now, let's fire one up!" I exclaimed as we headed for school. I loved getting high.

We smoked a fat joint, and when we pulled into the parking lot at school, some friends were hanging out in another car waving me to come on over. "Come on, Colin."

"I'll catch you later," he answered and disappeared into the school.

"Hey, Virginia! What's going on?" There was Patsy and Jennifer in the car smoking pot and drinking beer with her. "Oh, this is awesome. Let's go shopping!" That meant stealing.

"No can do. Not today. No money for gas. But my big brother, Tommy, bought us a case of beer. Wanna partake?"

"Would I say no?" I jumped in the car, and they plopped a six-pack of Budweiser onto my lap.

"Okay, so I was planning on bumming some change at the smoking area today anyway since we've got that Kiss concert coming up next week. I'll get us some gas money for tomorrow while I'm at it."

"Deal!"

Virginia was feeling "too good" to go in, she said.

It didn't matter that I was staggering a little, because everyone had already made it to class…except for Coach Severe coming out of his classroom at that moment for some crazy reason. I'm not making this up. His name really was Severe, and he *was* severe.

It was too late to dodge him or run.

"And where do you think you're going, young lady? I think you owe me detention for cutting my class two weeks in a row now." He had a firm grip on my arm now. I wasn't going anywhere.

I put on the "tough kid" devil-may-care face. "Whatever. How about I just take the paddling and get it over with instead?" I couldn't depend on Mom to pick me up from detention anyway, and it was a long way to walk home from school.

He produced "the paddle," a flat board with a handle carved on it, about three feet long. He told me to "spread 'em," which I did, bracing myself against the lockers in the hallway. I kept wondering when it would be over because as tough as I thought I was, this time it hurt like hell. But, of course, I couldn't let it show. In a very cool and collected manner, I went to the bathroom to catch my breath, then made my escape out the bathroom window.

Homeroom was over by now, and people were flocking to the smoking areas. Rebecca and her little gang caught me there.

"So what's this I hear about you hitting on my boyfriend?" She got in my face.

I felt my temper flaring up, which didn't take much, but I didn't want to get expelled. Granny was paying Rebecca's boyfriend to put shelves in mom's basement. I thought he was gross.

"I wouldn't have your stupid boyfriend!" I answered.

One of her two friends was twisting my hair with a pencil. "That's not what we heard."

"Well, I think I'll just follow you home on the bus and take care of this little problem," Rebecca warned. They walked away giggling, and one of them said, "Somebody's getting their ass beat!"

I was a little scared, wondering if I'd have to fight all three of them. She was a senior, and I was a freshman, but I'd been in plenty of fights before and never lost one yet. *They're probably just bluffing anyway*, I thought.

However, they did actually ride my bus and get off at my stop that afternoon.

It seemed everyone was at my stop that day. The five Poss kids were sitting up in the branches of the trees, cheering, "Fight! Fight!"

My neighbor, Debbie, was calling, "Beat her ass, Joye!"

And some boys who didn't normally get off at our stop were waiting at a distance, anxious to see what would happen. Colin wasn't there.

To my surprise, she walked right up to me and punched me in the nose, then in the stomach.

I wiped my nose, saw the blood, and lost my temper. It was a mad flurry of punches after that. I grabbed her hair with both hands and bashed her face into my knee over and over until she gasped, "Enough!"

I threw her to the ground.

"Kick dirt in her face!" Debbie yelled from the sidelines.

"Just for the record, I wouldn't have your dumb boyfriend if you paid me! You can have him!" I walked up the road to go home, just now noticing that my shirt was ripped. *Damn!* I thought. *That figures! The first week of high school, and I've already messed up my clothes.*

Debbie walked home with me, and as we passed her uncle's house, he stared from the front porch. He must have thought I looked a mess. Debbie was lucky. She had a mom and a dad who both had jobs in a sock factory. They had a nice house. Her dad even built her a playhouse that was a real cabin. Her mom was mean, but her dad was sweet. He always called my brother names like "Mr. Brown" and "Sparkplug" while they would look for arrowheads in his garden. Her family would all get together to play games on the weekends. They went shopping and bought nice furniture.

She had aunts and uncles and grandparents all living up and down our road too. When they all left for church on Sunday, my brother would go steal fish from their trout pond. They made home-made ice cream on the porch on Sunday afternoons.

The ugly words in my mind told me, *That kind of happy family life's not for you.*

I got cleaned up and changed so Debbie and I could walk to Johnny's Grill to play some foosball.

We sang over and over to the beat of our steps as we walked down Pisgah highway, "We must! We must! We must increase our bust! The bigger the better, the tighter the sweater, the boys'll be after us!"

Around dinnertime, Debbie had to go home, but the bikers and my other friends were just rolling in.

We'd get high and drink in the parking lot at Johnny's, and then order twenty orders of fries. When it was warm enough, we'd go climb the fence and swim in the public pool at night. But when it was cold, we all rode up on the mountain to a pull-off and built a bonfire. We did chocolate mescaline and purple microdot, and smoked hash. We drank a lot.

My second year in high school, Aunt Martha and Uncle Bernie offered me the chance to work and travel with them through Illinois and Indiana on the carnival.

For two summers during high school, I went to live in a travel trailer with Aunt Martha, Uncle Bernie, and their two young sons, Matthew and Tommy. Uncle Bernie worked as the safety inspector; he gathered permits, broke up fights, and generally managed things on the show. We traveled every week from town to town. It was long, hot hours on my feet, but I made good money working the shooting gallery and a coke pitch game. It may have been a little cramped, but it seemed wonderful to me to have birthday parties especially for me, homecooked meals, clean clothes, and a clean bunk to sleep in. They were very good to me. There were a couple of weeks when I didn't bring home much money, but Uncle Bernie would pay me a good amount anyway. They took me to the doctor and even to a chiropractor, on family outings to hike through Turkey Creek Park, or whatever they were doing as part of their family.

Aunt Martha cooked amazing food. The morning air was filled with the smell of buttery mushrooms cooking. They took me out for seafood dinner, treating me to my first Main lobster. It was so good! Old habits die hard, so I scoped out the live lobster tank, contemplating taking one home for later, but thought better of it, since it wouldn't be easy to carry it out stuffed in my underwear.

Once in a while, Aunt Martha and Uncle Bernie would go out and have me watch Matthew and Tommy.

Tommy was two then. He's in his fifties now, but he still remembers the terrible babysitting songs I sang.

> Did you ever see the "hearse" go by
> that made you think of the day you die?
> They wrap you up in a bloody sheet
> and drop you down about six feet deep.
> The worms crawl in, and the worms crawl out.
> They play pinochle on your snout.
> Your stomach turns a slimy green,
> then it turns to a thick whipped cream.
> You spread it on a piece of bread.
> And that's what you eat when you're dead!

Once I got back home to Mom's, I was able to buy, not steal, my school clothes, pay for enough oil to get us through the winter, and pay the light bill.

I thought the money I'd made would fix things, but instead, things just got worse.

CHAPTER 4

End of the Line

My brother was sent to Eckerd Camp for Boys for truancy, and I barely graduated high school. Despite Granny's warnings, I blew off a fully paid scholarship to Ringling School of Art in Sarasota, Florida. I was afraid of moving off there by myself, so I got married at eighteen instead.

Home in a Cow Pasture

He wasn't particularly romantic or handsome, but he liked to drink and get high, and most of all, he wanted *to keep me* by asking me to marry him. That was enough for me. His mother and dad bought us a trailer and parked it in the middle of their cow pasture. I worked at the local market part-time, and he worked occasionally as a brick and block mason when the weather was good, but it wasn't enough to pay the bills or buy groceries. Most of the time, he went without me to eat at his parents' house, and whatever time or money he had went to rebuild his custom-painted burnt-orange Dodge Charger.

"When are we gonna have kids, babe?" He was looking at my birth control pills. "I thought you were gonna get rid of these damn things. Aren't we gonna have a family?"

"Well, since we almost never have heat or a phone, I don't know how you can be always bugging me about having kids. We can't even take care of ourselves!" I was amazed at how stupid he was acting, although I guess he never had to take care of kids or even himself, so that would be my problem, right?

"You act like you care more about a phone than you do about what I want! I'm takin' off for the weekend with my buddies. We'll probably go camping and hunt down at Billy's cabin. Listen, I need my space. You need to go to your mom's for a while."

And with that, he was leaving me again to fend for myself. This had happened every few months for three years now. I was furious. This would be the last time he would tell me to leave. "You'd better be sure you want me to leave, because I'm not coming back this time."

"Yeah, babe, I just need to have some time to think things over. You know, hang with the guys for a while."

Maybe he didn't hear me right, or maybe he didn't think I meant what I said, so I repeated it. "Okay, but this one's for good."

"Aw, don't be like that now." He tried to kiss me, but I walked away.

He stormed out the door.

As always, he showed up a few days later at my mom's house, first cruising past the house like a tease, going on up the road and hitting the gas with a roar, as if to say, *Did you miss me and my fast, cool car?* In a few minutes, he came back and rolled slowly and dramatically into the driveway.

I was digging postholes for a makeshift fence to keep the rabbits out of a small garden I had planted in Mom's backyard. I was hot, tired, and highly aggravated by his arrival.

He fell to one knee and started crying. "I'm begging you to come back! I need you!"

To anyone watching this the first time, they would have fallen for his antics like a stone, but I had witnessed it one too many times. This time, he met my unleashed fury. I swung the shovel like a madwoman, barely missing his head with every swing, chasing him all the way back to his car.

"You sonofabitch! I dare you to ever step foot near me again!" My face was burning and sweaty, tears falling involuntarily down my dirty cheeks.

Mom finally came out of the house as he drove away. "I don't blame you one bit, sweetheart. I've seen him out with other girls."

Gee, thanks, Mom. Now you tell me.

* * * * *

In those days, I didn't know God, so I went to seek advice from a psychic lady named Darkus. She didn't know me from Adam, but for twenty dollars, she spent three hours telling me everything about everyone I knew, myself, and even what my choices were before my choices had come to pass. She suggested that I move to the city with a girl I knew from high school. I wondered who that could possibly be.

Homeless in Atlanta

Darkus's words cut to the core of my heart. Her words echoed in my thoughts over and over. *Three choices… No future with Mom… I was just an* object *to my first husband… Move on with the blond girl to a new place—a city not that far away.* An object! Well, at least that made a lot of sense.

I had no idea who this blond girl was until a week later, Kathy pulled up in her shiny new blue Camaro to Johnny's, my old foosball hangout. She walked in like she owned the place and tossed her long wavy golden blond hair over her shoulder. She was thin and pretty and had everything, it seemed. She dropped a quarter into the jukebox selecting "Margaritaville." We had gone to high school together, although we were never really close friends.

"Where've *you* been?" I asked.

"Hey, Joye! I've got a good job in Atlanta now. I've got a nice apartment in Dunwoody, but I'm looking for a roommate. You know anybody who'd be interested?"

"Yeah, actually, I need to get the hell outta here," I answered, "but I don't have any money."

"No money, huh?" She half smiled, thoughtfully. This was a foreign concept for Kathy. Her parents had moved to North Carolina when she was in the seventh grade from somewhere up north. I had been invited to a party at her house once, so I knew they were very well-off; better than any of the rest of us around here.

"That's not a problem," she answered. "You'll find a job there easy. I'm leaving in the morning. You can follow me there."

I had just gotten paid from my job at the Valley Market, filled my car with gas, and had fifty dollars left in my pocket. In my naivete, I thought, *Hm, I can do this. I have gas to get me there.*

"Okay, I'll meet you here." With the arrangements made, we talked for a while.

I had always been self-reliant, so I was excited to be away from my troubles and off on a new adventure.

The next day, with my clothes in the back seat of my old brown '65 Plymouth Fury that Granny had given me and fifty dollars in my pocket, I set off for Atlanta behind Kathy in the pouring rain. Miraculously, I managed to keep up with her after losing sight of her car several times, and we made it to her apartment in Dunwoody, Georgia. It was a nice suburb north of Atlanta. She showed me around the nearly bare apartment. It smelled of bug spray and dirty dishes, but it would be easy enough to clean with just the two of us.

"My mom and dad gave me a credit card so we can get whatever we need. Come on, let's go shopping!"

Kathy grabbed her purse and headed for the door. It had stopped raining now.

I was still tired from the terrible four or five hours trying to keep up driving in the pouring rain, and I didn't have money for shopping. I never was much of a shopper anyway. "No, thanks," I replied. "I trust your judgment." I laughed.

"Whatever, but I'm taking you out to the club tonight." And out the door she went.

She came home with a carload of kitchen gadgets and appliances, artwork, fancy curtains, and...a toilet seat cover with the whole matching set of towels for "decoration only"? *How unnecessary,* I thought. Then she proceeded to announce, "Your bed will be delivered tomorrow at noon. You can pay me back." She threw a huge plastic bag bundle of bed linen in the middle of my bedroom floor.

"You can pay half of everything, when you get paid of course, in payments. We'll work out the details." She continued. "Now, you sure can't wear those jeans with the knees ripped out and a ratty old T-shirt." She looked me over, up and down. "Wear this and let's go out." She handed me a tan silky shirt and matching skirt still in the dry-cleaning plastic cover. It was gathered and poofy, and it wasn't like anything I had ever worn before. For one thing, I never wore dresses. I felt uncomfortable and ugly, even though it was an expensive outfit.

Despite Kathy's attempts to get me into dresses and better-paying office jobs that I wasn't even qualified for, I landed a job at a convenience store within a week. Unfortunately, payday was every two weeks, and being held back a week, it was going to be well after the first of the month before I got my first check. It wasn't going to be enough to meet her expectations anyway.

The first of the month came, and Kathy wasn't cutting me any slack. She had no mercy.

"It's the first of the month, and your rent is due. Not to mention your half of the furnishings and what you owe me for your bed." Kathy's thin face looked angry and impatient standing there with her hand tapping her extralong salon-painted nails on her hip.

"Oh, like you really needed half of this stuff! I can't afford all this," I shot back.

"Okay, then, you need to leave. I'll get somebody else."

"Seriously?" I was shocked at her sudden decision but accepted the fact that I was being made to leave. Again.

I never stick around where I'm not wanted, so I went into my room to gather my things and put them in the car. Unbelievably, I had not one but two flat tires. *Oh great! Now I can't even drive to work on time!*

Kathy was already on the phone complaining to her parents about me, so once again, I was at her mercy and had to wait for the use of the phone.

Finally, I called Mom. It was a rare thing that she had a phone, so I felt that at least this time, I was in luck, but it rang and rang. *Please answer!* I thought, pleading. She finally answered. "Mom! The car has two flat tires so I can't get to work, and Kathy's kicking me out since I haven't gotten paid yet. Can you send me a bus ticket to get home? I promise I'll pay you back."

After a quiet pause, she answered, "Sweetheart, I haven't been working. Don't you know someone there you can get the money from?"

"No, but that's okay. I'll figure something out." I cut her off when she tried to explain and called into work, thinking I might try to walk. I explained my situation. To my great surprise, my boss JJ sent a guy from another shift to come get the tires fixed and bring me to work.

As it turned out, I went to the club that night after all. The guy JJ sent was a gay guy who decided to take me to his favorite club that night to watch the drag queens do their show. It was fabulous! A "girl" named Tina lip-synched a heartfelt rendition of the song by Melissa Manchester, "Come in from the Rain." The words touched my heart deeply, and I felt in some strange way that I was in exactly the right place. My new friends were passionate and understanding.

I lived out of my car for the following three months, frequenting the gay bars around town, until one night, an incredible thing happened. Lo and behold, I walked in, and there sat my best friend from high school!

"Colin! You're the doorman here?" Tears welled up in my eyes as we hugged. He was thin and pale like he hadn't slept or eaten in a long time. His straight brown hair had grown way down his back, and a long lanyard hung from his jeans pocket, adding to his hippie appearance. He seemed very odd and out of place as a gay-bar doorman.

"Oh my god! What are you doing here?" He held me by my shoulders at arm's length to look at me with concern and happiness all at the same time. His eyes were dark and watery like a sad puppy.

I told him the whole story about Kathy, and he told me how he was struggling too. He brought us drinks and pretzels from "his" bar, and later I shared microwave burgers and cigarettes from "my" store. We crashed for a night at his friend's house where everyone was getting high. The roaches there were overwhelming between the smell and the sound of their constant chewing and scurrying through the walls, so I was not inclined to stay there more than a night. However, we soon found out about an affordable apartment for rent right behind my work, so with great pride I acquired my first apartment at Curtis Garden just off Buford Highway.

Colin and his lover, Steve, moved in as roommates. It was a humble beginning. Upstairs, they had one bedroom with a separate dining area, partitioned off with Indian tapestries from World Bazaar for the "boys' room." It had ancient-looking hardwood floors which I loved, even if carpet *was* the "in" thing at that time. It had a tiny hallway of a kitchen, with teal-blue appliances from the fifties, no doubt, but it led to a back door with an incredible little balcony in the treetops out back. And all for $178 per month! Split three ways, that was sixty dollars each. That meant we had plenty to live on and to do as we pleased.

I slept on my clothes piled up on the floor as a cushion until I discovered the Chinese restaurant right behind my apartment building where I bought wonton soup for a dollar a quart. They threw away wooden crates in the back alley, which I could turn into a bed frame and all our other furniture. Crates with a door on top made a great dining table, along with crate stools. I made shelves for my clothes, and so forth. I turned one crate into an art table where I could paint and make some cash on the side. We acquired three iguanas and hundreds of plants from a neighbor moving out, so crates modified and screened in on the living room wall made a spacious cage for our new pets. We grabbed a white wicker couch and chair from beside the Goodwill donation box, so our little place really looked fantastic! We were home.

A guy named James was our neighbor. He lived next to the pool and had crazy parties going on every weekend where we drank and smoked all night and would jump off the roof into the pool. I remember guys making bets about who could swallow the most beer caps or cigarette butts. Crazy. One night, James got so wasted that he missed the pool and ended up in the hospital in traction.

We were all about having fun. One of our favorite hangouts was Piedmont Park, where we could rent roller skates for the day to explore the park's botanical garden, playgrounds, and trails. We flew kites, watched balloon races, and meandered through the massive outdoor art exhibits, but my favorite times were at the end of the day when we would settle onto an old blanket on the soft green grass to listen to a free concert with a bottle of wine or Colin's favorite, 100-proof Southern Comfort. Whether jazz or rock or folk, the Boon's Farm wine was sweet, and the weed was always plentiful.

The three of us got side jobs working for two Black girls who had started their own cleaning company, Michelle and Muriel.

We had stopped at the store down the street to get drinks.

Michele shouted the orders to Muriel over "Double Dutch Bus" blaring on the radio, while we sat in the back seat of their big green Cadillac, smoke boiling out of the tailpipe. "Just get waters for all of us. And did you remember the vacuum this time, Muriel?"

She nodded. "It's in the trunk! Well, I'll check." She got out to look. It was there this time. She went in to get the waters, and the manager came out of the store waving his hand in front of his face.

"Could y'all move your car? It's smoking up the whole store!"

"What the hell?" Michelle fumed as she yanked the steering wheel. Where's that dern sister o' mine?"

Muriel finally came back with five bottled waters in tow.

"You got the directions?" Michelle demanded.

"Yes," Muriel answered over "Brick House" now blaring on the radio.

"Then, heh heh, let's go!"

When we got to the house, we found that Muriel had forgotten the keys to get in. We all waited for her return, sipping our water and listening to "Fire."

We saved up and took summer trips every year to the Florida Keys. Life was pretty much perfect. Well, almost.

I got robbed at the convenience store twice. The first time with a tire iron to my head two weeks before Christmas, and again with a gun pressed to my forehead on Christmas Eve. After that, every time the bell over the door rang when a customer came in, I would begin to tremble, and my heart would race, so I quit the store and got a job waiting tables. I hated it, but the tips were good—some days a hundred dollars a day. My drinking increased, and I started doing quaaludes and cocaine. I moved on to another job cleaning houses and ended up working at a printing company in the mail room. That was when I met Doug.

Colin and I had gone to buy drugs at his house. When he answered the door, I was mesmerized by his piercing icy-blue eyes. He had thick long wavy brown hair down past his waist. He seemed almost bouncy with his easygoing manner as he led us into a sitting room where the walls were lined with record albums. Santana was playing. About six people were sitting around passing a joint and laughing and talking. He asked me if I wanted to go out to eat, so we started hanging out together all the time. We even went with Steve and Colin on our vacations to the Florida Keys, but he never said he loved me or called me his girlfriend. We were getting high all the time and dropping acid a couple of times a week. Neither of us had a car then, so I was walking across town to see him, and we were walking around town all weekend. One day, I was in his apartment looking at his books while he was out when I came across a whole section of books about witchcraft. *How interesting!* I thought, and I started reading about spiritual powers people could tap into by doing certain rituals and chants.

Meanwhile, back at the apartment, I had accumulated a total of five gay roommates in addition to a girl, my friend Ouida, so there was always something crazy going on there. I came home from Doug's one day to find Ouida waiting for me.

"Joye, there's s-something w-weird going on here!" She stuttered more than usual when she was excited.

She seemed upset, but I was tired from the weekend, and I wasn't in a very receptive mood.

"Yeah, what else is new?" I laughed.

Ouida was a loyal and understanding friend with the gift of insight. We called her Momma Ouida because she was the responsible one in the bunch.

"No, I'm s-so s-serious right now."

"What's up?" I made a conscious effort to listen to what she had to say.

"There's a d-dark presence here suddenly. D-do you feel it?" She tilted her head as if to get a better "signal."

And then I felt it too. All the hair stood up on my body, and a heavy feeling of dread swept over me. "We need to get out of here! We need to get out of here now!" We left.

When we came back home, one of the "party neighbors" had come to visit, and everyone was getting high. Somehow his lighter met with the jute wall hanging, and it caught on fire. The whole wall went up in a flash while everyone sat and stared at it. I grabbed it off the wall and began trying to smother the flames. As if in slow motion, the others joined in to help me, and we got the flames put out before any real damage was done.

That night, I relaxed in bed and was going through the mail. Mom had sent me one of her famous twenty-page letters and a bookmark with the 23rd Psalm that had a pretty scenery printed on it. The words touched my heart, and it seemed strange to me at that moment that I'd never tried to read the Bible, so I decided I would someday look this verse up. I decided to light a candle to scent the room and fell asleep. I awoke from a sound sleep sometime later to the shelf over my head on fire and crashing down on top of me! I still don't know how the candle caught the shelf above me on fire, but I got it put out. Another close call.

A few days later, I was driving in the rain when my VW bug was totaled as a car hit me on the driver's side from the turn lane. It pushed my car head-on into a telephone pole on the edge of a steep drop-off. I carefully picked out the shards of glass stuck in my head and babied two cracked ribs, but other than that, I was okay. Everyone was saying how I would have died for sure had the pole not stopped me from going off the concrete embankment.

Why this string of bad luck suddenly? I wondered.

Then there was my weight. I was very thin, only ninety-eight pounds. I kept losing weight, and it seemed like I couldn't stop it. I was starting to feel bad. I could barely climb the stairs to the apartment without losing my breath.

Smoking weed constantly and the two packs of cigarettes a day were catching up with me. I couldn't stop drinking, either. I had tried, but I always gave in "just this once." After all, I worked hard, and I really looked forward to my Bloody Mary brunch which started off my day of nonstop drinking. A little voice in my head was telling me that I was killing myself. *Am I going to die? How could I stop it? I don't think I can stop it...*

This brought me to the turning point of my life.

CHAPTER 5

Salvation

His Home in My Heart

My best friend Colin, his lover Steve, and I sat on the edge of the loading dock of Alco Printing Company where we were working, swinging our feet in the hot, dusty city air, smoking cigarettes on our break. We sat there sweating in the Atlanta midsummer heat as I admired the big black doughnuts I'd made in the parking lot from my little light-blue VW's entrance driving in that morning.

I bit my fingernails on one hand and picked at the holes in the knees of my jeans with the other. "I've been thinking," I said. "What if we were to save our money and go in together on a bomb shelter together? You know, in case there's a nuclear war."

Steve replied nonchalantly, "Oh, you don't have to do that." He took a deep drag from his cigarette, staring off across the parking lot and blowing the smoke out hard. We only got a ten-minute break.

"Why not?" I asked, blowing smoke rings.

"Well, someday, just before everything gets really bad here on earth, Jesus is coming in the Rapture. That's where He returns to gather up all the people who are saved into the sky with Him, and they'll be safe there."

Look, He is coming with the clouds, and every eye will see Him. (Rev. 1:7)

I was shocked. "What? I went to church as a kid, and I never heard that!"

"Yeah, it's true. You can look it up for yourself," Steve answered. It was already time to go in.

We all flicked our cigarette butts into the back lot and got up.

"So how do I get saved?" I asked.

Here I am! I stand at the door and knock. If anyone hears My voice and opens the door, I will come in and eat with him and he with Me. (Rev. 3:20)

"I'll tell you what," he answered, "I'll take you this weekend to meet my mom and dad in Opilika, Alabama. They're both Baptist Sunday school teachers. They'll explain everything to you."

"Okay, but why didn't you tell me this before?" I asked, still amazed that I had never learned of such an important event from anyone ever before in all my life!

"You didn't ask." He gave a flourishing hand gesture and smiled at me with his handsome grin under his thick dark-brown mustache.

For God so loved the world that He gave His one and only Son, that whosoever believes in Him shall not perish but have everlasting life. (John 3:16)

On July 17, 1984, at the age of twenty-four, I attended Philadelphia Baptist church where I nearly ran to the altar at the end of the service to "get saved." I solemnly raised my right hand and prayed a simple prayer, repeating after the pastor, "Lord Jesus, please forgive me for my sins and save me. Come into my heart and into my life, and by Your Holy Spirit, give me the power to turn away from my sin to follow You. I believe that You died on the cross to forgive my sin, that You rose from the dead, and that You have gone to prepare a home for me in heaven. Amen."

**We all, like sheep, have gone astray, each of us
turned to his own way; and the Lord has laid
on Him (Jesus) the sins of us all. (Isa. 53:6)**

A home of my own. That had been my dream for so long, but
I had given up without even realizing it; I had gotten so sidetracked.
The hope I'd had so long ago had faded far into a long blur of days
and nights that had turned into years of hunting for the next fun
thing to get into.

Doug had said something about how I was "boring," which had
made me so mad that I had recently broken it off with him. For once,
I didn't care what some guy thought.

All my dirty secrets; the molestation, the date rapes, and all
the twisted encounters with sex, drugs, and drinking; the sign "Sex
Object" that I had imagined was written across my chest, where men
were usually looking first all these years, fell away like dirty old blankets of shame. I was forgiven. I had a new identity now, which was
"Child of the King."

**As far as the east is from the west, so far has
He removed our transgressions from us. (Psa.
103:12)**

Suddenly, I had a new clarity that I didn't know existed, which
opened me up to new thoughts and ideas flooding my mind like
a wave of wonder and excitement. Now I realized that this unseen
world of good and evil is real, and that there is a continual battle for
the souls of everyone on this earth.

I went back to work at the mail room feeding the label machine,
but now I had a new perspective about every part of my life. Instead
of the impending loneliness and constantly thinking about hanging
out with friends, I was thinking productive thoughts like, *People are
basically three parts: the spirit; the soul, which includes mind, emotions,
and personality; and the body. What would be a healthy diet? What are
the right exercises for me to do? This is kinda crazy, I know, being that I
weigh less than a hundred pounds. I need to learn how to overcome evil!*

There's so much to learn! There's a whole world of good things to explore, another invisible world that we cannot see… Nevertheless, it is so real! I did have a lot to learn.

I was afraid that if I lost any more weight I would just die and disappear forever.

When the Spirit of truth comes, He will guide you into all truth. (John 16:12)

I knew for sure that I wasn't thinking up all this stuff on my own. I had a new best Friend, and His name was Jesus. I couldn't see Him, but I *knew* He was there with me. I can't explain it. I just knew.

The wrenching loneliness and emptiness that had haunted me all my life was what, I believe, led to the need for "fun" friends who lived to party, as I did, numbing myself into a state where nothing mattered. I knew it was affecting me to the point of no return, and I had tried to stop, but up until now, I had been unsuccessful. Miraculously, the cravings for alcohol and drugs that I was consuming on a regular basis had left me completely. It was like an open window of opportunity with a refreshing breeze that I knew would only last as long as I stayed obedient to the Spirit's calling. But there were influences everywhere around me, and I knew I had to get away from it all. As much as I loved Colin, my best friend for over twelve years, and Steve, and all the good times with my other friends and roommates, it was time to say goodbye. I packed up whatever I could in a little old Mazda I'd just bought with the last bit of money I had, since the VW was totaled. The Mazda was literally held together with electrical tape.

Steve offered to ride with me to Mom's in North Carolina and meet up with Colin there later. Mom was living in her trailer again where it had been moved to the farm. Nana and Grampa had stayed in it while building their house up Warren Creek.

We headed out on the four-hour trip up very steep mountain terrain. The engine was racing, but the little Mazda struggled to climb at twenty miles an hour, then ten miles an hour, then slower until we were barely moving.

"Should we stop and ditch some of this stuff in the back seat?" I was frantic, wondering what we would do next. Would we be stranded there on the side of this mountain in the middle of nowhere? I always thought I had to be self-sufficient and figure everything out on my own, but this time, Steve knew we had God on our side.

"Oh, ye of little faith!" Steve proclaimed, "His angels are pushing us up this hill right now!"

For He will command His angels concerning you to guard you in all your ways; they will lift you up in their hands. (Psa. 91:11)

I didn't say a word and just kept my foot on the gas. Finally, we made it to the top of that mountain and all the way to Asheville and finally Candler, North Carolina, to the old farm.

When we got there, we parked at the road and climbed the grown-over stone steps that led to a muddy path up to the rotted wooden stairs to the trailer. Mom greeted us from her spot at the table, with the ever-present coffee in one hand and cigarette in the other. She was surrounded by the familiar stacks of boxes and piles of dirty dishes. Steve looked around but was too polite to say anything about the mess. I was embarrassed, even though I was accustomed to this reaction from people and usually just ignored it. We talked for a while before Steve and I teamed up to get a fire going in the woodstove and clean the kitchen as best we could.

Steve and I cleared an overstuffed chair in the "dining area" and laid blankets beside it on the floor to rest. There was no food and no heat. I gathered some more wood to keep the woodstove going. It was time to find another job and find it fast. I took the first thing available, cleaning nineteen rooms a day at the Ramada Inn in Enka. I scrounged for change and came up with enough for a loaf of bread, some peanut butter, and some gas for the car, but it was the first of August, and I had one payment left on the car for ninety-eight dollars. It would be weeks before I got paid from the new job, and my old self said, *Just blow it off... That car's a pile of junk anyway!*

However, the old guy I'd bought it from was nice enough to let me leave the balance that I couldn't pay at the time to a few payments, so my new spirit spoke to my heart about doing the right thing. "Lord," I prayed, "I'm doing my best, but I don't know how I'm going to come up with this last payment. Please help me."

It just so happened that the next day, I received a forwarded letter in the mail from a utility deposit refunded to me to the amount of forty-eight dollars, which was totally unexpected. I was very tempted to spend it on groceries, but something didn't feel right about that. Even though eating peanut butter sandwiches was getting old fast, I held on to the forty-eight dollars.

The next day, Nana came walking up the path from behind the trailer. I had just gotten up from sleeping in my spot in Mom's over-stuffed chair and stepped outside for a breath of air.

"Oh, there you are!" she said, almost in a whisper. "I was coming to see you… Where's your mother?"

"Inside, sleeping," I answered.

"Well, I know your birthday's not until next week, but I wanted to give you this ahead of time." She slipped a folded-up bill into my hand and patted it. "Don't say a word of this to anyone!"

"Absolutely! Thank you so much, Nana!" I hugged her tightly, thinking how she and Grampa had changed so much from the days when they went off and left me places. I had been praying so much for her and Grampa and everyone in the family to be saved.

Believe in the Lord Jesus and you will be saved, along with everyone in your household. (Acts 16:31)

I wondered if maybe my prayers really were making a difference. Being unsentimental as she was, she hurried off, back up the path to the house.

Tears welled up in my eyes as I opened up the bill, which, to my astonishment, was fifty dollars. The exact amount that I needed together with the forty-eight dollars to make my final car payment! "Thank You, Jesus!" I whispered.

**My God will meet all your needs according to
His glorious riches in Christ Jesus. (Phil. 4:19)**

Grampa had also mellowed in his old age. He checked my car
for me, adding oil and filing the spark plugs to keep it running so I
could get to work. Steve bought me a bag of tortilla chips and a jar
of salsa.

I was going to the little Methodist church that Granny took
me to when I was a kid, and someone there had set me up for an
interview with a job at a government printing company starting at
eighteen dollars an hour! I was ecstatic at how God was providing!

With my first check from my cleaning job, I stopped by
Burgerland to grab a burger. It was a restaurant that I had worked
at years ago when I was married. There I saw a familiar face walking
in the opposite door. It was John, who had been the line cook there
back then. We greeted each other and got to talking.

"What're you doing here?" I asked.

He answered in his Greek accent, "Oh, I don't work here anymore. I just dropped by to see my old friends here at the restaurant."
It was owned by his Greek friends. "I have my own painting business,
and honestly, business here isn't too good with all the rain we had
lately, so I think I'm going to head back to Florida. The weather is
good there, and so I stay very busy there year round. What're you up
to?"

"I'm staying at my mom's right now, but hopefully I'll get my
own place soon. I may be getting a really good job soon." He knew
my mom. It seemed like everyone did.

"Would you like to come to my house for dinner?" He told me
where the house that he was renting was.

"Sure," I answered, trying to conceal my excitement.

His house was nice. It was immaculate. He cooked us steak,
baked potatoes, and corn on the cob for dinner. I couldn't remember when I had eaten like that. It seemed like nothing ever tasted so
good. He liked to work out. He didn't smoke and didn't drink. He
even had his own business. He seemed to have it all together.

I liked him. I cancelled the interview for the government job, and two weeks later, we were in Fort Lauderdale getting married.

His proposal: "I'm gonna marry you."

Something old: After much deliberation and a full-blown argument, he agreed to tow my old Mazda with my few belongings inside.

Something new: Everything. A new relationship. A new culture. A new home. A new adventure.

Something borrowed: Our wedding rings were borrowed from a friend's plastic-baggie collection and returned afterward. My dress was taken from off the rack at another of his friend's dry-cleaning store and returned afterward also.

Something blue: Me. I was missing my old friends, my music, and my family and wondered what I had gotten myself into.

Steve and I had parted ways, and Colin later found out that he had AIDS.

The Home with No Screens

We started out with a thousand dollars which he had saved. It was enough to make a down payment on our own house, or even a duplex as an investment that would pay for itself, but he wanted to rent a place instead. He hustled up a few quick jobs immediately, which was quite impressive to me, and we moved into a little one-bedroom house with no furniture. I was no stranger to humble beginnings, so we made a table out of an old door set on five-gallon paint buckets and used paint buckets for stools. We were painting outside in mid-August, so the heat made me sick to my stomach and dizzy. I was exhausted but trying to prove myself. The heat didn't seem to bother him at all. There was no air-conditioning, so we had the windows open all night, and in the morning, we were covered in mosquito bites. Even my eyelids were swollen with mosquito bites.

Now, I had been reading my Bible faithfully, and I know beyond a shadow of a doubt that **God is love (1 John 4:16)** and **He works all things out for my good (Rom. 8:28)** even if I couldn't see how that was possible right now. This was all just a test of my faith, and I did feel like Job right about now, so I would seek solace in going into the bathroom and praying quietly, kneeling beside the tub. The door was a slated door that made my kneeling slightly visible to my husband's watchful eye.

"What are you doing in there?" he demanded.

"I was just praying," I answered.

"Are you becoming a nun or something?" he asked sarcastically.

He huffed with disgust, but I knew what I had to do. I had to stay close to the One who would get me through this. I had made a promise to follow Jesus and a sacred vow by way of marriage, and I planned to stick it out no matter what.

**He rewards those who diligently seek Him.
(Heb. 11:6)**

Home at the Triplex

We eventually moved from that house to a triplex where my first daughter, Sotiria, was born. I stayed home to take care of her. I was spending a lot of time memorizing scripture and fasted for forty days for the guidance of the Holy Spirit, following the example of Jesus.

Little Sotiria was named after John's mother. We called her the shortened American version, Ria. So small and fragile and beautiful. I called her my little hummingbird as she sweetly hummed in my arms. I had a dream one night while she was still breastfeeding that I was lying down in the back of a wagon pulled by horses. It seemed so real. I was wearing a long dress, and I could even feel the sun's heat beating down on me. I could hear my baby crying but felt helpless, like I was too sick to move.

That week, my breast was exceptionally tender, and I thought it was due to the skin being cracked from nursing, but when I woke up that day, I had a high fever and could barely stand on my feet. John drove me to see our family doctor, Dr. Limperis, who checked me and prescribed an antibiotic.

"You know," he said to me, "if this had happened to you a hundred years ago, you'd probably have died because they didn't have antibiotics in those days." *What an odd thing for him to say*, I thought, considering the dream I'd had the night before. Thank God, the Lord works through medicine and doctors!

By His wounds we are healed (Isa. 53:5)

The Parsonage Home

We found a very small one-bedroom house, roughly the size of a two-car garage, that was an old parsonage right next to the Faith Church of the Nazarene, for a very reasonable rent. It was one bedroom that we divided into two bedrooms just big enough to fit the beds into. That's where we lived when our second daughter, my beautiful Mary, was born. We named her Mary Jane, after my mother. I called her my little lovey-dovey, because she was so affectionate and loved to snuggle on my chest.

When she was only a few days old, I had tended carefully to her belly button, assuming it would fall off and heal perfectly, but that was not the case. To my surprise, it got very inflamed, and though I tried ointments and alcohol, it just wouldn't heal. I took her to the pediatrician, who gave her an antibiotic and prescription ointment and told me it would take a few weeks to heal, but he wanted to check it again in a few days. I went home and applied the ointment and gave her the medicine, but to my amazement, the next day it looked terrible! It was swollen and dark colored, like a bruise! I was so worried, but I would have to wait for John to come home, which I knew would be late. It could be days before we could get her next appointment. So I prayed. I knelt beside her crib, crying, and simply said to the Lord, "I know You can heal her, Lord!" and recited a scripture I knew:

**Behold, You are the Lord, the God of all flesh;
is anything too hard for You? (Jer. 32:27)**

When I looked up, her belly button was perfectly healed! It was truly a miracle! When I took her back for her checkup in a few days, the doctor was astonished and said he'd never seen anything like it before!

The girls weren't old enough to start school yet, and John didn't want me to leave them in day-care, so I couldn't work. I had no money to spend or give, so I gave my time and got very involved with the Nazarene church; the cleaning, the visiting, the choir, the teaching of Sunday school and children's church, Vacation Bible School, the bus ministry, and the church board. It was a small group of believers, about thirty or so, and we were a tight-knit group of friends that seemed more like a family. John even got baptized and was involved with the bus ministry. We also went to the Greek church sometimes.

However, it was a bad neighborhood with the high school just up the street, and in a busy part of the city. Our house was broken into, so, to remedy that situation, we came home from a friend's birthday party with two puppies, sister and brother, half black Lab and half golden retriever. Missy was Ria's dog, and Freddy was Mary's dog.

Those were good days filled with busy and rewarding hours of playing a part in the saving of souls.

But my happiest hours were at night, holding the girls both on my lap on the swing that John made for us out of a board and some rope, under the carport, singing them to sleep. The night air was warm and the traffic far enough away to be a steady background noise. I liked to make up my own happy lyrics to the old nursery rhymes:

> There was an old woman who lived in a shoe.
> She had so many children, she didn't know what
>   to do.
> So she fed them all spaghetti with buttery garlic
>   bread.
> She read them bedtime stories and tucked them
>   into bed.
> And kissed them on the head.

Many happy nights, they fell asleep in my arms on that swing.

We took trips to Greece in the summertime to see John's family, and Mom came to visit us.

It wasn't always easy, though. Mary was two. Ria was three. They would fight over Barbie shoes or one thing and another all day long. A shrill resounding "Stoooop!" punctuated the days continuously. I would separate them and say, "Ria, say sorry," or "Mary, say sorry," and "Mary, say, 'I forgive you,'" or "Ria, say, 'I forgive you.'" They would stay in time-out for five minutes, then be right back at it again. One day, it drove me to the edge. I went to the back window to pray. I pressed my face up to the glass, tears welling up from frustration. "Lord," I pleaded. "I don't know where I'm gonna go, but I'm coming outta here!"

I heard the still, small voice in my heart. *Why don't you go to work at the preschool where you can take the girls with you?*

My sheep listen to My voice. I know them, and they follow Me. (John 10:27)

I looked out my window up the street and remembered there *was* a really fancy preschool just up that street. But then I thought to myself that I should go to the other school nearby called Sun Fun. It was small and not so expensive looking. That would be more my speed. Again the nudge came. *No*, my heart said. *You should go to Maginnis Preschool!*

Okay, the fancy one it is, I thought.

Immediately, I got myself nicely dressed, got the girls nicely dressed, and headed up the street to the Maginnis school to ask for a job.

When I arrived, a pretty woman came out to greet me. It was Mrs. Maginnis herself. I introduced myself and the girls. I told her I was looking for a job.

"Well, isn't that something!" she exclaimed. "Just this morning, I prayed and asked God to send me someone, and here you are!"

I worked full-time at minimum wage, and the girls both got to go for free. Soon we got a VW bug and were able to go on outings to the parks, the beach, the libraries where we could check out free books and movies, and to the thrift stores for cute, inexpensive clothes and toys. What happy times to treasure!

John was a self-employed house painter, so when he had work, we had money, but sometimes things were pretty lean. One year, on Thanksgiving, John hadn't had any jobs in a while, so we were down to a bag of rice and a jar of gravy. But something wonderful happened.

It was a beautiful sunny day, and the girls were in the big grassy side yard, feeding the pigeons that hung around the church, as they often did.

"There they go!" Mary tossed her blond hair, pointing with her little finger as the flock of pigeons took flight around the roof of the church and flew in a big circle to come around and land to get the bird feed that she and Ria were tossing on the ground. Ria clapped her little hands to get the feed dust off, and stood like a little model with her long straight brown hair and her hand on her hip to watch excitedly.

"Mommy, what's on that one's leg?" asked Ria, leaning to observe a white pigeon.

"Is it hurt?" Mary added, climbing up to stand on the chair for a better look.

I looked hard at the one white pigeon that we had never seen with the others before. It had something tied to its leg. "That's a good question, sweetie," I answered. "John! Come quick!" I called.

He came out, and we showed him the new pigeon.

I said, "I wonder if it's a note or what."

He set right to work and fashioned a kind of crate trap to catch the white pigeon. He propped one side of the crate up on a stick with a string tied to it. The girls sprinkled some more seed under the crate, and we all stood back, anxiously watching as the white pigeon got closer and closer and finally stepped under the crate. John pulled the string, and the crate fell, trapping the pigeon unharmed.

John carefully untied the string on the pigeon's leg.

Ria and Mary bounced up and down with excitement. "What is it? What is it?"

To our surprise, it was twenty-two dollars, exactly the amount we needed to go to the Morrison's restaurant, where we normally went every year for Thanksgiving dinner!

"Will you look at that!" I exclaimed. "God has done a miracle!"

"Thank You, God!" We all praised God for His faithfulness.

When John released the white pigeon, she flew into the sky, and we never saw her again.

Our little Sarantis, named after John's dad, was my handsome blond and blue-eyed boy. We called him Randy, for a shorter American version. He was quite the surprise. I thought I had a case of stomach flu until the nurse convinced me otherwise. His sisters already knew, though. They had prayed for a baby brother.

Just before I got pregnant, my mother went to see a medium, who told her that I would get pregnant but that I would lose the baby. Outwardly, I dismissed it because I had no intention of getting pregnant at that time. However, I had been to see Darkus years ago, so I held this in the back of my mind, thinking about how she had known so much about everything in my life and how everything she said had come to pass.

When I found out that I was pregnant, this medium's words kept ringing in the back of my mind: *she'll get pregnant, but she'll lose the baby.* About the third month, I started having some bleeding, and I thought, *she'll get pregnant, but she'll lose the baby!* I went to the clinic that I had been going to as soon as I could, and the doctor told me to stay off my feet or I might *lose the baby!* I went home feeling more afraid than ever, trying to stay off my feet, but it was nearly impossible with a house to take care of and two little girls to run after. I prayed, begging God to help me, but the bleeding and cramping kept getting worse and worse. One day, I got down on my knees and prayed, sobbing, "Lord, I know we don't always get what we want, but I'm asking You to please help me to have this baby…a healthy baby!"

Immediately, a scripture verse number came to my mind: *John 10:10.* But I hadn't memorized that one, so I hurried to look it up in my Bible.

The enemy comes only to kill, steal, and destroy, but He (Jesus) has come to give us life and life abundantly.

I knew the Lord had spoken to me! That verse was for me! Every time the bleeding came back, I recited that verse out loud, "For He has come to give us life and life abundantly!" Within two weeks' time, the bleeding stopped completely, and in nine months, our son was born beautiful and healthy. I called him my little eagle because he had risen above the circumstances by God's great power and love. I know not all prayers are answered in that way, but I do know that when we surrender whatever concerns us and trust God with whatever the outcome may be, He will always bring about the best result, whether it may or may not seem like it at the time. Sarantis was my brave little eagle who rose above the voices of this world and the circumstances in this life that said he wouldn't make it.

The Haunted House on Hartley

In today's society, we don't really think about evil spirits lurking around, but there are at least twenty-five accounts of Jesus casting out demons in the Bible. I was still a young Christian and young in my faith, so I didn't recognize them as much then, but I can assure you, they do exist today.

Fort Lauderdale had gotten terrible in our neighborhood. The Nazarene church had closed down, and I was afraid to start the girls in public school there, so we moved up the coast to the little town of Palm Bay.

We drove the dusty back roads of old broken grassy paving lined with sweet-smelling wildflowers until we found a house for rent that would allow us to have our two dogs, Missy and Freddy, outside.

It was a very modest three-bedroom house painted white with white carpeting. There were vacant lots all around us, so we had quiet and privacy. I cut small trees from the pine woods that surrounded our little house for fence posts and bought cheap wire to fence in the backyard for Missy and Freddy. John built them a nice roomy doghouse. It finally seemed like a dream come true, with the exception of the white carpet!

Aunt Martha came to visit us from Chicago several times, taking us to Universal Studios, Wet and Wild, and SeaWorld. She bought inline skates for all three kids to go to the school-sponsored skate night every month. What fun we had with her!

I had gone to visit Mom in North Carolina just a short time after Nana passed, and Grampa was in a home for the elderly, so I went to visit him.

Uncle Paul had taken care of them both in their home on the old farm. "He's not going to be able to talk to you," he said. "Your grandfather has Alzheimer's really bad, and I guess they keep him drugged up there at the home. He probably won't recognize you."

"I know, but I don't know when I'll get a chance to see him again," I answered.

I drove to the home and walked into a screened porch with people rocking and sitting around. I noticed that they weren't talking with each other, but they all stopped to stare at me as I walked by. I smiled at them and kept walking to find out where Grampa's room was. They also assured me that he was on sedatives and probably would not wake up or be able to hold a conversation.

When I sat by his bed, I held his hand and had barely begun to pray, when he opened his eyes and looked right at me.

"Grampa?" Silent tears rolled down his face, and I asked him, "Are you hurting?" He squeezed my hand and nodded yes. Of course, I had meant whether he was hurting physically, so I was just about to call someone to come help, but then he answered clearly, "I miss your Nana!"

"You know you can be with her. Would you like for me to pray with you?"

He nodded yes. "Pray after me, Grampa." We prayed the sinner's prayer, and he said every line after me in a clear voice. When he repeated "Amen," he closed his eyes and went back into a deep sleep.

I was so thankful that the Holy Spirit had prompted me to go see him.

On the way out, one woman on the porch asked, "Where are you going?" and held out her hand as if she wished she could go too.

I don't remember what I said to her now, but now I wonder if I should have asked her if she wanted to pray so she could go to heaven too.

Aunt Martha offered to sell us her part of the inheritance of Nana and Grampa's farm with the creek in North Carolina for a very good price, ten thousand dollars for 6.18 acres. I had talked John into buying it, which he agreed to, thinking it would be a good investment opportunity. I was thinking more along the line of retirement in the beautiful mountains that I loved. But now we planned to look for a piece of land near us in Palm Bay where we would finally settle and build our own home! All the years of hard work and saving every dime was finally bringing us to a place where we could settle for good.

I started dreaming of our new place and began drawing elaborate house plans, mostly for fun. I drew all kinds of plans over and over, perfecting each one. I imagined a modified A-frame of stone and timber frame with a grand bedroom and full bath upstairs in the peak, complete with a fireplace and balcony. The downstairs was spacious with bedrooms for each of our children and an extra bedroom for company with a fireplace in the living room. There would be a beautiful glass greenhouse room for dining and grilling off the kitchen, with herbs and fresh vegetables growing in planter boxes. Best of all, at the front of the house there would be a round tower library made of stone and filled with all my favorite books. A staircase would wind along the library wall up to the art studio at the top. I would drive my sporty new dark red car down a long winding driveway to the middle of a rich green forest of huge trees. I saved every magazine picture or article that depicted the lovely home that I had in mind. I let my imagination go wild, all the time knowing that my dreams may not be practical, but it was so much fun to think about! We would more likely have a more modest home. But it would be *our* home! For our *happy family!*

John dreamed of having a big yard "like a jungle" of tropical fruit trees. I liked his dream too.

We found an acre and a half of land in the next town of Grant and began looking at model houses. We settled on a spacious four-bedroom house with an office and formal dining room and a large back porch that could be closed in. It featured two master bedrooms, one of which could be used for when his parents came to visit. I got to pick out the hardware for the kitchen. They looked like leaves on a vine…so pretty! And the kitchen countertops were a beautiful dark green with gold marbling. This would be our dream home, where our sixteen years of hard work and saving would finally pay off. John decided on a builder, and soon the building of our new home was underway!

One day, I went to visit our next-door neighbor, Becky, where we lived at the rental on Hartley. She was taking grapevines from the woods and making Christmas wreaths out of them to sell.

"What a great idea!" I told her, checking out her handiwork hanging out on the back porch. We could see my backyard from there.

"Yes, well, I thought it was ingenious of you to build your own fence out of those little saplings! Just look at all the money you saved!" She was a heavy woman, pretty, with long dark wavy hair, and a nervous habit of biting her lip. She added, looking toward our backyard, "Have you noticed anything *unusual* about the house?"

"Not really, except that little Randy is terrified to go into the kitchen. He swears there's a huge alligator in there! And there's a lot of really big spiders, like the size of my hand! You know I really hate spiders, and I've been killing them every day! But, after all, this is Florida, and the woods no less! So…" I gave a shudder and wondered, "Why do you ask?"

"Well, there was a very strange lady who lived there before you moved in. She used to have fires in the backyard and chant and bury things. You know, like a witch." And then, as if to lighten things up a bit, she added nonchalantly, "She was a school bus driver."

"Do you think she really was a witch?" I asked.

Becky laughed nervously. "I guess you could say that."

After that, I noticed a lot more things started happening.

Our struggle is not against flesh and blood, but against the rulers, against the authorities, against the powers of this dark world and against the spiritual forces of evil in the heavenly realms. Therefore, put on the full armor of God. (Eph. 6:12)

CHAPTER 6

A New Beginning

Over the years while the kids were young, I had taken some Bible study and counseling, art, and writing courses that landed me a job that I loved as the teacher for elementary art and a combined class of third- and fourth-graders at First Christian Church Academy. The church paid for my schooling as a teacher, along with giving me a small paycheck, and Ria, Mary, and Sarantis got to attend with no charge for tuition.

When I found out Mom was sick again, I knew I had to go help her get to and from her chemo treatments, though it was against John's wishes. It was Christmas break when we left for North Carolina. My son, Sarantis, was two years old, my daughter Mary Jane was eight, and my daughter Ria was nine when I transferred them into school there to finish out the year.

It was a very special but brief few months in early spring for us to spend with her. I never regretted that decision because while we were there, Mom had asked to go to church to be baptized. We drove to the biggest Baptist church that I knew of in the area, First Baptist Church of Asheville. At the end of the sermon, the invitation to accept Christ and be baptized was given. A long row of people lined up, and as they were baptizing people, everyone clapped, but when they called my mom up, and she came up out of the water, the Holy Spirit went through the crowd like a roar of thunder! They didn't know my mom from Adam, but they clapped and cheered and stomped their feet until I thought the building would fall down! Such emotion swept over me that I couldn't help but sob happy and grateful tears.

In April, Mom lost her fifth and final battle with cancer.

Nana and Grampa had passed away, so Uncle Paul lived in their house now, and Mom had lived in a small borrowed camper trailer across the road. Uncle Paul had always kept an eye on her to make sure she was okay and did things like run a long extension cord to her little trailer so she could have power. Paul would leave his basement unlocked for her to use the water and his washer and dryer. She was a night owl and always loved to keep all the lights on, which in years past would have made Grampa furious at her "wasting electricity." However, after the kids were in bed, I loved to go sit up with her. This was her quiet time to stay up dreaming and planning the wonderful things she would have liked to do. In one of our long, late-night conversations there, she had told me her plans to plant wildflowers in the whole yard and paint little signs to go over her dogs' houses with their names on them.

When Mom got too sick in the last stages to take care of herself, God provided a wonderful friend of hers, Frances McFarland, whom we called Bunny. She brought Mom into her home and stayed by her side to care for her in her last days when I didn't have any way of doing that.

A week after Mom had gone to be with the Lord, the kids and I were all sleeping together at my Uncle Paul's house in his extra bedroom. Ria, Mary, and I woke up, and we all sat up in our beds at the same time that morning.

Little Mary started with, "I dreamed about Grandma! She took me for a ride in the creek in a little boat. She was wearing a funny outfit—red jeans and a red-and-white striped shirt. The stripes were big stripes going up and down like this." She motioned up and down the front of her.

Instantly, I thought about an old photograph of Mom in that outfit! Mary had never seen that picture of Mom in her twenties wearing, as she had described to me, her "favorite outfit," but it was the very same one that Mary was describing now!

Then Ria said, "Mom, I dreamed about Grandma last night too! She took me to where she was, and it was beautiful! Her whole front yard was filled with wildflowers. She had a big two-story house, and every light in her house was on! Then she took me around the back of her house to show me how she had painted the names of her dogs over the doors of each one of their houses!"

Ria didn't know how many times I had seen my mother buy wildflower seeds to plant, or how many times I had listened to my grandfather curse when he saw her leaving every light in the house on. Ria didn't know how she sat with me during those all-night conversations and told me about how she had planned to paint her dogs' names over their doors!

I believe that was the Lord's way of letting us know that Mom was okay and still very much a part of our lives, forever in our hearts.

Many years later, my husband, Steve, dreamed that she had met him in a restaurant wearing a fur hat, which he described being just like the one that she wore a lot when she lived in New York City, but he never knew her or about that hat either. And then one day, Steve and I went to breakfast at a new place in Melbourne, Florida, where we lived called MiMi's Café. When we walked in, he exclaimed, "This is where your mother and I had coffee together in my dream!"

That same year, my friend Colin died of AIDS. Colin had also prayed for salvation, but it broke my heart to see my best friend become an unrecognizable skeleton.

When we got back home to Palm Bay Florida, I started my new full-time soldering job at MC Assembly. I was hurrying from work to pick up the kids from school. The sky was black and ready to burst with the usual afternoon thundershowers that hit in early summer every day right about pickup time. We got home in the pouring rain and ran inside the house. By now, the white carpet was a hopeless mess.

"Everyone, go shower and get out of those wet clothes! Now! I'll go start dinner."

When I walked into the kitchen, a black furry spider as big as my hand turned its body to look at me from the corner of the kitchen ceiling. I have always been terrified of these creatures, and this house had the worst ones I'd ever seen. I could spray and set off bombs, but they just got worse and worse. I got the broom and whacked it as hard as I could. I opened the garage door to sweep it out, and there between the piles of laundry, two brown wolf spiders were playing with a dryer sheet, tossing it back and forth and throwing it up into the air! Disgusting! They ran away as I stood there thinking about how to kill them, so I went on over to grab the dog food and went out to feed Missy and Freddy.

Every day, I watched Kenneth and Gloria Copeland on *The Believer's Voice of Victory*. They taught on faith mostly. I knew I had faith because when I asked Jesus to come into my life, I knew He brought His faith with Him.

Today, Kenneth explained a vision he'd had. "Now in this vision, there was a gigantic dragon. I mean, this thing was huge! I saw this sword nearby, and I was thinking to myself, I'll use that to kill this thing, but when I put my hand on it, it's just like it had a mind of its own, and it just took me with it. I didn't lift it or anything! It just went right for the heart of that dragon and killed it! And that's just the way the Word of God is if you'll use it…"

The word of God is alive and active. Sharper than any two-edge sword, it penetrates even to dividing soul and spirit (Heb. 4:12)

I finally got the kids to bed with leftovers on the stove waiting for John.

I lay on the couch, fighting sleep. The ceiling always looked like it was moving. The barrel-style chairs began swiveling around by themselves. My heart was pounding, and I was frozen with fear.

I had tried several times to cast the demon, or demons, out of that house. I would say, "Evil spirit, I cast you out in the name of Jesus!" but things only seemed to get worse. I thought about something Doug had said about going around the perimeter of the house with salt. I tried that too. At the time, I didn't realize that **divination, sorcery, witchcraft, and casting spells are detestable to God (Deut. 18:10, 11)** and **that man should not think he will receive**

anything from the Lord; he is a double-minded man, unstable in all he does (James 1:7, 8).

I started quoting, **1 John 4:4, "He who is in me is greater than he who is in the…"**

I was interrupted by Ria's sleepy voice as she stumbled into the living room. "Mommy, something is touching my face when I close my eyes."

I hugged her. "Go back to sleep. Your angels are watching over you all the time, sweetie." I sat with her until she drifted off again.

When their friend Serina came to spend the night, they complained of "the headlights of a bus" shining in the girl's bedroom window, waking them up.

Every night for three years, I had terrible, vivid dreams that I was hiding from someone trying to kill me. Mary and Ria often had nightmares too.

John had grown very quiet and seemed increasingly depressed and angry. I was wondering why he wasn't coming home before ten or eleven at night. Whose house needed painting at that time of the night? I grew suspicious, thinking he might be seeing someone. He asked me once if I had put poison in his food. It seemed like he was always mulling something bad over and over in his mind.

I was astonished at his even thinking such a thing. "How could you say that? I'm on *your* side! I would *never* do such a thing!" We sat in silence for a few minutes, and I felt it was a good time to get things out in the open.

"I *will* say that I'm not happy. We need to do something to bring our relationship back together. I don't know what I'm doing wrong… Would you consider a date night out together maybe once a month? We need to talk about this!"

He wouldn't answer. He just slurped his soup.

We had a conversation one day when he told me he married me just to have children because he thought I would be a good mother, but he had never loved me. After eleven years of marriage. I cried for three days.

The ugly little font in the back of my mind popped up once again with *You will never be able to follow or live your dreams. You will never have a happy family life.*

When I went to seek counseling from my pastor of the church I was attending, I learned that he had run off and left the church and his wife with three young children for a young woman who had just joined the church. Had the whole world gone insane?

John wasn't an affectionate person. He never slept with me. He made a bed out of blankets on the living room floor. Soon after my request for a date night, John came to the bedroom and woke me up in the middle of the night, about three in the morning. He grabbed me out of bed and practically dragged me outside to the side of the house. He started banging me against the wall, bruising my forearms, yelling in my face, "Who are you f——?"

"Have you lost your mind? How can I be seeing anybody! I go to work, pick up the kids, and come straight home!" I was confused and shaking. I was angry too.

Finally, on Easter Sunday, he pushed me into my car while the kids stood watching through the front doorway and told me never to come back, yelling threats as to what he'd do to me if I did. He told the kids that I didn't love them anymore and just wanted to screw around. He threatened to take them to Greece to let his mother raise them and I would never see them again.

Stunned, I drove to a nearby park and sat for hours wondering what to do. I had no one to turn to except Jesus. As a wife, I thought I had done everything I was supposed to.

I needed to refocus on who the real enemy is here, the devil. I wasn't fighting John. We were under attack and didn't know how to handle it. John said the Lord's prayer every morning, but obviously, our words weren't enough.

This evil spirit that had taken over was now throwing me out of my own home, and worse yet, had taken my family away! All our hearts were wounded beyond anything I had ever imagined possible.

I thought about the story in the Bible when the disciples asked Jesus why they couldn't cast out a demon, and He answered, **"This one comes out only by prayer and fasting" (Mark 9:29).**

Hadn't I prayed? Hadn't I fasted? Hadn't I done everything I knew to do?

Maybe Jesus meant that we need a certain level of spiritual maturity that comes only in time by a continual closeness to our heavenly Father; in prayer, and a level of self-sacrifice; fasting, not from food necessarily but a sincerity from the heart, seeking to please Him, and Him only, in everything we think and do.

I wondered, *Maybe we just weren't spiritually mature enough to handle this deep level of evil. Maybe it wasn't anyone's fault. Maybe it was just something we had to get through and keep trusting God for some reason we might never know.*

I felt I had failed at everything that was important to me—my marriage, my kids, my faith.

John followed me to work. The belts and tires on my car were getting cut every week. The guy at the recap tire store wanted to know who had it in for me.

I went to stay temporarily as a roommate with a friend I had met at work until I had enough money to rent a small cheap apartment, but my rent was still more than I could afford at $850 a month, with me making only $6.50 an hour.

When John and the kids moved into the new house, the kids said they heard footsteps in the middle of the night, like heavy boots, walking up the hall, and when they got up to see who it was, no one was there. *Was an evil spirit responsible for our divorce? And did it follow John to the new house?* There were so many things I didn't understand. I just had to trust God, no matter what, that He would work everything out for our good somehow.

Home at the Pines Apartment

Now the world is set up to distract us from God, usually when things are easy, but especially when things become too hard for us. We tend to look more at the problems than keep our focus on the truth of God's Word; that He will provide what we need if only we'll turn to Him in our times of struggle.

Or in fear, pride, and impatience, we can try to provide for ourselves.

Sarantis was with me about half the time, and one time I walked with him to Kmart to steal a jacket for him when it got cold because I had no money. I applied for food stamps and could only get sixty dollars a month for groceries. It just wasn't enough.

Every time I tried to see the kids, it was a violent screaming scene, even in public, when I encountered John. He would tell them I had abandoned them, which to me, with my past, was the worst possible thing I could ever do, in my mind. Mary went to stay with a friend doing God knows what, and Ria, who stayed with me, had always been a gifted student, but she started skipping school and acting out. They had as little to do with me as they could. We were all angry and hurt. Little Sarantis suffered going back and forth constantly between his dad and me. He had a rough time in school.

My children were my whole world. I cried every day at work and wondered if or how this hell would ever end. My body constantly felt weak and shaky. Terrible thoughts constantly bombarded my mind while exhaustion took its toll. I started having health issues and gained weight. I had to work as many hours as possible just to keep afloat.

Most of the time, I felt too numb to pray, but one day I said, "Lord, I know You'll find a way someday to make this all up to me."

Our lead at MC was a quiet, patient man named Steve Frost. Manufacturing circuit boards was something new for me, but he taught me all about running the machinery, how to inspect the boards, and how to solder. He was respected for his congenial attitude and knowledge by all the people in his department. I personally respected the fact that he never came on to me like some of the other guys whom I worked with did. He was married but never talked about his personal life. He listened mostly.

I had memorized and written out 1 Corinthians 13 with a Sharpie on the picnic table where we took our breaks. It was to remind me that love was still out there somewhere. Seeing the words made it seem tangible in some strange way.

"Is that a poem?" Steve asked.

"No, it's from the Bible," I answered, and I noticed that he acknowledged it without judgment. I tried one of the canned yams I had brought for lunch. I had gotten them from the donation box, and they were all I had left to bring that morning. "Oh! Yuck!" I exclaimed. They were terrible.

"You can have one of my cookies," Steve offered. "Chocolate chip." He held one out for me to take.

I was starving, so I took it. "Oh my gosh, these are delicious!"

"My dad bakes them all the time," he added. "Listen, I didn't want to tell anyone about this just yet, but I know you won't say anything to the guys. I think I may have a really good job offer, and I might take it."

We had been working together for eight months. When he said he might be leaving, a funny thing happened. My heart leapt and sank all at the same time, and I felt a sort of panic. I didn't say anything, but all afternoon and all night, all I could think of was Steve. But how much crueler could it be that I had discovered these feelings for someone who was married? I was afraid to talk about it to God, ashamed of my feelings and trying to resist and ignore them. I knew it was wrong.

I couldn't wait to see him in the morning to get the details. I tried to be cool about it. I waited until he came to inspect boards across from me at the end of the machine.

"So, any idea as to when you'll be going…?" I asked, secretly hoping that by some miracle, he'd changed his mind.

"Well, it's a good drive from my mom and dad's, so that's something to think about, but the money is worth it, I guess."

"Your mom and dad's?" I was a bit confused.

"Yeah, I've been staying with them for a couple of months now. Things didn't work out for my wife and I."

"I'm sorry to hear that," I lied. And then I blurted out, "I don't want you to go!"

He sat quietly for a few minutes, then asked me, "Would you like to go to breakfast at Denny's with me tomorrow morning?"

After breakfast, we watched the sunrise at the beach together. We did that often. He wrote me little love notes at work inside my work glove where only I would see it. He brought fresh flowers and cards for no special reason to the apartment often and wanted to see me every chance he got. He wrote so many love poems for me that I keep them in boxes to treasure. I was his "Pookie," and he told me I was the most beautiful woman in the world and how he loved me, every single day. He was always looking for some way to inspire me to follow my dreams. Once, he gave me a pad of graph paper, and when I asked him why, he answered, "To draw your dream house." I drew it so often that he told me that if I used all the paper of the plans I'd drawn, it would be enough to build it! He bought me a folding easel full of paints and a ten-pack of canvasses when he found out that I liked to paint. He was always bringing me gifts.

His song to me was "I Love You" by Moody Blues.

He turned down the other job offer. Our first date was in November, and we got married that next April on Melbourne Beach, Florida.

I took enough out of my 401(k) to put down on a house. We bought a thirty-year-old ranch-style fixer-upper that had four bedrooms and two baths, in a modest neighborhood. It was a terrible sight with its dark brown wood and bright red brick exterior, old windows, and the dark brown metal front door rusted up to the knob. The yard was mud with all sorts of things sticking up out of it, and big ugly stumps of old bushes grew along the front, too close to the house. It was a little scary to be undertaking such a project, but the size of the house could work for us and our five children, the price was right, and we were up for the challenge. I borrowed an additional $750 from Aunt Martha for the closing costs, to which she exclaimed, "How did you know that's exactly what I had saved?" Well, I didn't, but God did!

We applied for credit cards from Home Depot, Sears, and Walmart and set right to work.

CHAPTER 7

Let the Adventure Begin

The House on Eastman

A man stood at the entrance of Rainbow Lumber and pulled back a tall beat-up metal gate to let us drive through. We were proudly driving our new black station wagon with our new little red trailer from Harbor Freight bouncing along behind.

I was mesmerized! "Have I died and gone to heaven?" I whispered. Steve smiled. I was so excited. "Look! There's a mountain of bathtubs!" I pointed. "And a mountain of toilets!" We looked at each other and giggled. Neither of us had been house shopping together in…well, ever, so this was a grand experience, to say the least. The dirt trail of a driveway twisted and turned through acres of piles and piles stacked high with kitchen cabinets, sinks, doors, bike racks, siding, and every reclaimed household item imaginable.

"Check out this cultured marble sink!" Steve measured the bathroom sink; it was pale green mixed with off-white swirls. "It's the right size! What do you think?"

"Oh my gosh, it's gorgeous! I love the color…but how much do they want for it?"

The man yelled, "Twenty bucks," nonchalantly.

We gave each other an excited glance, and Steve loaded it onto the trailer. We left with sinks and cabinets for both bathrooms. The existing ones were the originals from 1972, rusted-out sink shelves held up at the corner with a two-by-four. We rescued beautiful new white-trimmed windows to replace the ones across the front of the house that were rusted shut…including a floor-to-ceiling bay window for the living room!

Steve's mom and dad came to visit, and his dad helped us replace all the windows. I chipped away the top rows of the old red brick to fit the new windows in, and painted all the rest of the brick with beige and brown tones to wash over the bright red. Our new siding was light beige. We planted a beautiful garden in front of the bay window with a red and white flowering oleander. Steve's kids, Jenny and David, brought us a beautiful ficus tree for the front yard, and the grass began to grow in nicely.

David, Jenny, and Sarantis were in the back seat of the station wagon as we drove down the highway one day.

Jenny read the signs we passed along the way. "Look! Old Fart Trailer Park!"

We all laughed, since the sign read "Old *Fort* Trailer Park."

Steve stared intently at a huge yard sale across the street.

"Ha ha!" David laughed. "Dad's checking out that yard sale like it's a hot babe!" They laughed but couldn't wait to get out of the car to look for themselves.

"This light is so beautiful!" I picked it up carefully by the heavy black wrought-iron chain. It was a stained-glass swag lamp to hang over the dining room table. For only five dollars! Unbelievable!

"Can we get these games?" Sarantis asked. Two dollars for all the games they had. In the car they went. We were all happy as could be.

Steve bought a really nice picnic basket. *I'm sure he's planning something romantic*, I thought, smiling to myself.

Our home was full of everything we had ever dreamed of and more. We put up a twenty-four-foot pool in the backyard, got a great deal on a hot tub, and even bought an older camper for just $1,800.

We closed in the carport to make it a garage.

Then the storms came. In one year, we had seven hurricanes hit one after the other. We were out of work twice, for two weeks. The kids were home with no electricity for AC in 100-degree weather and no water because it ran by an electric pump. We weren't able to cook. The kids were teenagers now and could eat a ten-pound bag of potatoes with two chickens and a gallon of milk for one dinner without any leftovers.

We had to replace all the insulation in the attic, and the soffits had all blown off the house.

The water heater and AC system had to be replaced, and the kids needed uniforms for school.

The list went on and on.

We had maxed out the credit cards, so we looked for ways to earn more money. We both worked overtime at MC Assembly and took on cleaning jobs at a school, the dog track, and Club 52. I had an additional job cleaning a bank during the week. We picked up scrap with the little trailer to sell. We had a renter to stay in one of the bedrooms. We picked up furniture and other items from the side of the road on garbage day to fix up and sell in yard sales. We refinanced the mortgage. We sold the camper and the pool. We sat at the flea market for several sweaty weekends trying to sell pillows made from an abundance of clean foam discarded at work, but that was a bust.

We had to get rid of the station wagon, and Steve had gotten a little two-seater convertible Geo Metro. The AC didn't work, but at least Ria could drive it to get to her classes.

David, Steve, and I climbed down out of our other car, an old, faded, pinkish, purplish Amigo with big tires… I hated that car! We were exhausted and aching all over after the early morning cleaning routine. We dragged ourselves into the bedroom and fell into bed.

Rattle, rattle, rattle, rattle, rattle, bark! Bark! The dog next door was right outside our window, dragging a heavy chain back and forth. Tears welled up as I thought I'd never get enough rest ever again.

That afternoon, Steve called me from the garage. I went out to find him up on the ladder.

"I was looking to maybe put in a duct system out here to turn the garage into another room, and I found this." He poked at the ceiling, and powder came falling down.

"Termites?" I asked in disbelief.

"It's a lot of them," he answered. And without even getting down from the ladder, he added, "This, I'm afraid, is the straw that breaks the camel's back." He hung his head sadly.

Apartment Living

We let the house go into foreclosure and tried to consolidate our bills to a manageable level. We sold most of our things and rented first a house, sold our things to downsize again, then got an apartment. When the rent went up the next year, we moved again into another apartment.

I was devastated at losing our house, but I tried to look on the bright side. We were slowly getting out of debt and not working as much. The pool was already cleaned, the grass already cut, and we could actually stick to a budget without a lot of extra expenses popping up all the time for maintenance. But even though the dust was beginning to settle, it wasn't ours. As always, it was just temporary. I tried to console myself as I walked up the sidewalk after work each day. There was a certain large crack in the sidewalk that I would look at and think, *This isn't my sidewalk, so I don't have to worry about fixing it.*

I couldn't find a church that I wanted to go to. I didn't listen to Christian music or listen to preaching anymore. I had drifted away from God. I felt like in the whirlwind of life, I had let Him down. I wasn't doing anything to build His kingdom because I had spent all my time and energy trying to build my own, and maybe He had forgotten about me too, I thought. The kids were grown and had all gone their own ways. I didn't feel as thankful for everything we had accomplished as much as I did disappointed and resentful for trying so hard and, after all that we'd been through, for what we didn't have.

One sunny afternoon, as the breeze was coming up and it began to cool down, I took our border collie, Jesse, out for a walk by the canal near our apartment building. I looked across the canal at the neatly manicured homes on the other side. Someone was having a family barbecue in their backyard. The little kids were running around laughing, someone was grilling, and the adults were visiting on the back patio. Though it was close enough for me to smell the delicious meat grilling and hear their laughing and talking, that kind of life seemed like a million miles away for me.

With tears in my eyes, I prayed, "Lord, how can it be that all these other people can have a home and a happy family, but not me? I know You, **God, can do anything (Matt. 19:26)** and all the houses and **everything in the world belongs to You (Psalm 50:10–12)**, so why can I not have a home and my family together? You promised to **never leave or forsake me (Duet. 31:8)."**

Many times in the past, I had heard His answer as a still, small voice in my heart, but this time there was only silence.

God had spoken to my heart a long time ago about meditation, but I thought of it as an Eastern-culture type of thing and didn't really understand what it meant concerning God. Just sitting quietly and still seemed like a major waste of time to me, not to mention practically impossible for me to do.

Be still and know that I am God. (Psa. 46:10)

On a quiet day off, I visited the library. Looking down the rows for something interesting to read, I came across a book called *Paramahansa Yogananda: Autobiography of a Yogi*. I've always had the dream to write and illustrate books for children, so I read a lot of children's books. I had recently read a story by one of my favorite children's authors, the famous Roald Dahl, called *The Wonderful Story of Henry Sugar*. It's about this man who learns that he has incredible powers by way of meditation and does amazing things for people with his gift. So the word *yogi* made me curious, and I checked out the book.

Though I didn't agree with all of the doctrine, it turned out to be an unlikely answer to prayer. It opened my understanding to a new way of knowing what it means to surrender.

I learned that meditation, simply put, means putting aside all distractions, fears, dreams, plans, wishes, past, and future. It means relaxing completely, mind in the present. It means waiting on, and focusing only on, the presence of the Holy Spirit. It means consulting Him first and involving Him in every detail of life. I realized that this was the missing piece of my "faith puzzle" that I had never fully grasped. Maybe because surrendering our selfish wants is not a super popular concept in this instant-gratification society. But it most certainly is a vital component to our spiritual maturity. And, obviously, God is more interested in our spiritual maturity than He is in quickly getting us that dream house or dream car.

I went back and had another talk with God, this time humbly on my knees. "Lord, I'm so sorry that I haven't been as close to You as I once was," I began. "I guess I'm just really tired, and I need to rest somewhere that feels like home. Somewhere I can *stay awhile*. But I know that You love me, and You watch over me. You know my heart, and You know what I need and when I need it. I choose from here on out to trust You with my life. I can't change my circumstances, but somehow, I know You'll do what's best for us. Here and now, I give my desire for a home and my family over to You, and I'll be happy with whatever You bless us with from now on."

Vinu's House

Now you would have thought that when Steve's boss, Vinu, offered us the cutest little house for rent-to-own that it would have been the answer to my prayer. But God still had some surprises in store for us.

I loved that house. It was a little three-bedroom, two-bath house nestled in between two wooded lots, protected by the trees from storms, set in the curve of the road on a quiet back street. It had vertical wood siding painted a lovely shade of sage green and a cozy timber framed-in front porch. The porch swing was framed by a large yellow flowering Mandeville growing up the lattice to make it a nice little hideaway for reading a good book. It even had the same front door that I had chosen for John's house in Grant, with a beautiful cut-glass window. Steve bought me a Meyer lemon, mango, and tangerine tree for the backyard. We enjoyed having the family nearby and celebrated Thanksgiving and Christmas in our spacious sunroom dining area off the kitchen.

I had my heart set on having a pretty white wicker chair to go on the other side of our front porch, but we didn't have the extra money to buy one. Just for fun, I took a picture of one that I liked, cut it out, and glued it on the porch of a picture of our house. I took it to work to show it to the ladies in my department.

My friend, Lola, laughed when she saw it. "Girl, you're crazy as you wanna be!"

I laughed at me too, but that week as Steve and I were driving to Walmart for groceries, a glimpse of something in the ditch caught my eye as we turned the busy corner at the red light.

"Quick! Pull over!" I was so excited that he pulled over right away into a nearby parking lot so I could jump out of the car to go check it out. I waited for a break in traffic and crossed the street to see my beautiful white wicker chair, legs up, down in the ditch, barely visible from the road. When I got it out, nothing was broken. It was good as new. I imagine someone had dropped it off their truck when they were moving and didn't notice or couldn't find it. Thank You, God!

Vinu's deal was verbal that we could live there, renting his house for two years to decide if we wanted to buy it. In the meantime, he asked us to do all the repairs, which made me want to get a written contract, but we could never seem to pin him down on that.

Home on Highway 357

Steve received a phone call from his dad one day. "Hey, Pa."

"Hi, son. Everything okay with you guys there in Florida?" Pa asked.

Steve answered, "Well, we just got the news that, after three years, Vinu finally told us he's decided to keep the house and just rent it. It looks like we're gonna have to move again. And after all this work we did. Joye's upset about it. I'd like to try and buy us a place if we can."

"You guys ought to move up here to South Carolina!" Pa jumped at the idea of us going there. "That's what I was calling to talk to you about, anyway. Ma and I are having a rough time here right now. You know I've been sick, and I'm having a hard time keeping up with this place. You two are sure welcome to stay here with us. We have plenty of room—two spare bedrooms. There's lots of jobs here. We'd love to have you."

"That's right! Come on!" Ma yelled from the background.

Steve was quietly thinking it over. "I'll have to discuss it with Joye and see."

"Well, let me know. We could sure use your help."

"Okay. Love you, Pa."

"Love you too, son."

Steve hung up, turned to me, and asked, "What do you think about moving to South Carolina?"

"Well," I answered, surprised. "I always wanted to move back to North Carolina and build a place there on our property, but I guess South Carolina is close enough. But what about the kids?"

"You know, they're really not kids anymore. David's off in Indiana, and Mary and Sarantis are off in Orlando going to school. Ria and Matt are married, and they have their own family now. They're settled in their house with the girls. Jenny and the kids'll be fine. She and her mother-in-law are helping each other out."

I knew it was true, but I needed to pray about it. After a few days, the Lord gave me confidence in my heart that it was the right thing to do.

We sold most of our belongings once again and moved in with Matt and Ria for a year to save up and get Steve through the back surgery he needed. What a precious time to spend with my daughter and her little family! I was able to see them buy and remodel their first home and watch my granddaughters blossom into beautiful young women. How I loved morning conversations over coffee with Ria on her front porch.

The girls giggled out front while they raced their remote-controlled cars with Matt, whirring up and down the road and back into the driveway.

Daisy, their little dachshund, excitedly chased lizards and methodically checking every plant where they could possibly be hiding, while Ria scrolled on her phone to check her emails.

"Oh, here's one from my friend who just opened her own yoga studio. I'll check out her new website."

Ria's a yoga enthusiast, and she got me interested in it also.

She read the website to me. "Featuring singing bowels? Surely, she meant bowls!"

We roared with laughter. When I finally caught my breath, I added, "Yeah, if the bowels are singin', don't come ringin'!" And the laughter started all over again.

When we moved to South Carolina, we had planned to live with Ma and Pa for five years and work as much as possible to save up and buy our own place nearby so we could help them out. They were in their eighties now. When we arrived, the grass was tall, and the kitchen needed cleaning. The flower beds were all grown up in weeds and dotted with Ma's collection of faded gnomes that had gotten knocked over with time. I was excited to set out right away putting my painting skills to work on the neglected gnomes and spent all winter freshening things up. Ma and Pa made certain that we had warm clothes for the winter and bought Steve and me beautiful new winter coats.

Living with Ma and Pa was a fun adventure. They both have a sweet and lively spirit and love to joke around. Steve took us all out to eat often, driving the winding country roads as we laughed and talked along the way. One day as we drove over the train tracks, I read a sign at the side of the road that said, "Caution! Raised manholes ahead!"

Pa made a terrible face and turned to look at us in the back seat with big eyes, yelling, "What!"

We all rolled with laughter.

It was such a blessing to get to know them and see Steve enjoy being there for them.

We both got jobs right away. There were a lot of jobs out there. At first, we took night jobs that were available, but it was hard to sleep in the daytime after working days for so long.

And then there was Pa. *Bang, bang, bang!* He beat as hard as he could on the bedroom door, waking us both from a sound sleep.

"What do you want me to do with these clothes in the laundry basket?" he yelled through the door.

Steve started looking at houses in the area on his laptop. I guess the five-year plan was out.

"Hey, Joye," he called. "Come take a look at this."

The first thing I saw on the screen was a tall, three-story house with green siding, a deck off each of the three floors, set in a backdrop of huge trees. There was even a curved slide on a dock at the lakeside! The price read $199,000. Under two hundred thousand for a lakeside home? Regular houses in the area were going for more than that! I had worked in real estate, and I knew the price was good. I couldn't believe my eyes as we scrolled through the pictures of a brand-new kitchen with dark wood cabinetry, stainless-steel appliances, and marble countertops. The spacious master bedroom was on the second floor with a large walk-in closet and a separate laundry room. The bathroom was very large also, with the same dark wood cabinets and marble countertops, a large shower, and a big corner garden tub. There was light hard-wood flooring throughout the whole house. Three flights of stairs wound up to a spare room on the third floor with a half bath and closet which could be converted to a shower for company. All three decks faced the lake. It was magnificent!

"Let's go take a look!" I begged.

We jumped in the car after calling the realtor to meet us there. The mile-drive to the house seemed so surreal. I wondered, *What could be wrong with it? It just seems too good to be true.*

CHAPTER 8

The Lake House

Just a few blocks from Ma and Pa's, the GPS took us off the main highway. We drove down a side street, the quiet countryside dotted with nice but not fancy houses, all the way to the end of the road. The house was only a mile away from Ma and Pa! There it was at the end of the road, standing like a tall sage-green castle, the lake sparkling behind it in the afternoon sunshine. A little creek wound through a grove of giant poplars next to the house.

We met Charlene, the realtor, in front of the house, introduced ourselves, and went inside.

After we looked at each of the rooms, we came back downstairs, where Charlene calmly waited in the dining area.

"What do you think?" she asked. "I have some other houses in the area if you want to look some more."

"No, thanks, I love this one!" I answered, gazing up from the bottom floor through the middle of the stairway to the third floor.

She looked at Steve for the final approval. "What Pookie wants, Pookie gets!"

We all laughed.

I knew we couldn't drag our feet on this one. I had already decided this was it. It was the week of my birthday, and with his VA loan, Steve put five hundred dollars down. Everything went smoothly, and we bought the house.

We soon filled it with all the things we loved. Steve had his big-screen TV and his easy chair. I gave my bird feeder a fresh coat of brown paint and hung it right outside the dining room window. Pa made me a beautiful craft desk for the extra room upstairs. We got a new gas fireplace that instantly comes on at the touch of the remote, and I bought a pretty sign to go over the fireplace that reads "Stay Awhile." Ma and Pa gave us a bench swing for the deck off our bedroom, a barbecue grill, and a big shade umbrella for the bottom deck. I put up shelves to enjoy all my little keepsakes from Steve and the kids. I hung pictures of the whole family on "the wall of fame" in our living room.

And Now, For the Dream To-Do List….

- Getting the driveway paved and herringbone pavers would be nice!
- Put in a shower and a closet to turn the extra room upstairs into a guest room.
- Install a pretty front door with stained glass, to expand the front porch, and add on an ivy-covered pergola.
- Have stairs built off the back deck and create a garden with a long dining table and hanging lights for outdoor parties in the backyard.
- Change the small shed for a bigger one as a workshop for Steve with room for storage, and get rid of all cardboard boxes and piles/clutter in the house!
- Install doors under the stairway to add storage space.
- Maybe a nice gate and a permanent car cover for both cars.

I had big plans, I know. Even though I've heard people say things like, "God isn't interested in every little detail of your silly life," I believe that He loves us beyond our comprehension and would very much like to be involved in the little things, the big things, the serious things, and even the silly things. After all, the Bible says our very hairs are all numbered! What a concept! I try to talk to Him or at least think to Him about everything throughout my day. My list certainly didn't fit my budget or expertise, but I'm a dreamer, and that's where the prayer basket comes in.

My friend Diane weaves the most beautiful baskets. I was so fortunate to receive one as a gift, a little oval basket about six by eight inches with no handle. It is woven of muted greens and pinks among the natural reeds, which became the place for my special prayers. I reached into it to retrieve a three-by-five index card. *Lord*, I prayed, *this is Your house, and I would like very much to take good care of it for You. What verse would You have me write to remind me that this home is a gift You have so graciously given us, and You will provide us with a way to take care of it?*

I began by sanding and staining the back deck, as we had good weather combined with a three-day weekend off from work.

Three days went by, and as I was reading my Bible, this verse made item no. 1 on my list, the driveway, come immediately to mind.

The path of the righteous is level; O upright One, you make the path of the righteous smooth. (Isa. 26:7)

I can't do it. He'll have to make a way.

A Happy Family

Steve fashioned a teepee over an air mattress in front of the big windows in the dining area where Naia could spend cozy hours reading, and Ma provided the most beautiful paisley drapes to cover it. The girls were coming to visit! Naia and Callie slept in the teepee. Ria and Mary took the room upstairs.

It was a flurry of activity getting settled when they arrived. Then the five of us took off on a hike across the beautiful wooded hilltop to Ma and Pa's to play dominoes. Steve opted to drive over and join us once we had arrived.

"How about some freshly baked chocolate chip cookies?" Pa asked, bringing out a huge plate piled high.

I looked out the back window to see my granddaughter perched in the top of the wisteria growing over a large arbor over the birdbath. "Callie!" I called out the back door. "You want to join us for dominoes?"

Her beautiful extralong blond hair fell around her as if she were a princess in a nest made of flowers. "Nah, I'm good." She smiled. I knew she was enjoying herself. She loves being outdoors in nature, and she loves her quiet time to herself.

I thought it was sweet that Naia gave up her reading to join us as we gathered at the table with our pigs in blankets, snacks, and Pa's delicious cookies. Mary and Ria proudly wore the scarves I had given them at our little get-together. *Here we are!* I marveled to myself. *Having our very own family game day!*

Soon after, Sarantis came for a visit. He wanted to have breakfast on the deck, but it was raining. However, that evening the rain stopped, and we stood on the back deck in the cool of the evening.

He loves to do funny voices and said in a little-kid voice, "Wow! Will you look at that!"

Then he added in his regular voice, "I don't think I've ever seen this many fireflies in my life!"

It really was amazing, and I knew it had made his visit special. *Thank You, Lord*, I prayed.

Ice on My Windshield in December

Steve is always buying good books for me to read. A Japanese writer by the name of Masaru Emoto wrote a book called *The Hidden Messages in Water*. He had done studies on the effect of human consciousness on the molecular structure of water. There were pictures of how ice crystals formed when exposed to the positive vibrations of uplifting music or words…*and even thoughts!* Also, there were pictures of crystals exposed to music, words, and thoughts of a negative nature. The pictures of the water turned to ice crystals while exposed to the positive were quite symmetrical with beautiful and intricate designs, and, fascinatingly, the ice crystals derived from the negative were clearly not beautiful but haphazardly and oddly shaped. I wondered, *How can this be? I think this experiment is scientific evidence that our beliefs, thoughts, and words are shaping the material world around us... Science that is a perfect example of faith!*

On a cold Saturday morning on January 9, 2021, a week or so after reading *Hidden Messages*, I was up early while it was still dark outside, getting ready to drive to work. When I stepped outside to start my car, I saw that Simone's car was parked on the left, and Steve's car was parked to the right of my car. Their cars were both covered in a clean white solid blanket of frost. To my amazement, my car in the middle was covered completely with the most beautiful design in the frost, like a magnificent frozen feathery white paisley! I wondered, *Is it because I always listen to Christian music while traveling to and from work each day? Was it God reminding me that He is with me?*

God knew that I would need Him now, more than ever.

Working on a Saturday

After my wonderful icy surprise, once again I drove out of my driveway to go to work on the last Saturday in January. If you recall in the first chapter, this is where our story began. It was freezing cold at 5:00 a.m., and I felt a bit jealous that my husband was still snoring in bed. *He hardly ever has to work on a Saturday!* I grumbled to myself. I wiped the sleep from my eyes then took a sip of my coffee as I drove up the road into the frigid darkness. The warm liquid felt so good to my sore throat, though my head was a bit woozy. I didn't have time to read my devotion that morning or say my prayers before heading out. But then there was the long, forty-five-minute drive to work, so that was plenty of time to talk with God, I thought. Though this morning, feeling as bad as I did, my heart really wasn't in it. I was so stiff and sore that it was an effort to even drive.

Steve had bought me the book *Creation Frequency* by Mike Murphy, which had inspired me to make positive affirmations part of my daily routine.

"Thank You, Lord, for this beautiful day, for my loved ones, and even my job." I smiled at such an ironic prayer and how I was **"calling things that be not as though they are" (Rom. 4:17)**. "Thank

You for my husband and family, my home, and my nice new car. And for my coffee!" Saying these words softened my attitude a bit, and I added, "I love You, Lord." I couldn't help but think about all the things that I had to be grateful for. I broke a smile as I remembered that first wish so long ago as a little girl, for a home and a loving, happy family.

It was still dark when I pulled into the parking lot at work. I dragged myself up the sidewalk and scanned my badge in at the door. Just inside, I lifted my safety glasses and pulled down my mask for the temperature sensor, installed ever since COVID began. I waited for the green bar to pop up on the screen to tell me whether I had a fever or not.

Boop. The computer screen showed green. Good to go.

I was so miserable. My throat felt like knives cutting every time I had to swallow, and the chills were terrible. And on a Saturday at that! I was thankful for my heavy coat, even though it didn't feel like it was enough to keep me warm. My body was aching so badly, but the drive was too long to go back now. I soldered my cables and got through to twelve noon when I finished for the day. Finally, time to go home. We normally didn't have to work on a Saturday, but thankfully, it was usually just six hours if we did.

I was thinking to myself as I drove the miserable forty-five-minute trek home, *Dear God, if Steve and I are both sick, who's going to help us? Well, I can always count on David. He's been really good to us, helping out around the house and all.*

David had gone to jail in Indiana for ten months for multiple DUIs before we moved into the house on the lake. Despite my apprehension at his coming to live with us, considering his tumultuous past with drugs and alcohol, David and I had been writing letters every week while he was in jail. He seemed like he had changed, and Steve and I knew he would need help to get back on his feet. I love David. I had to give him a chance. After all, I do understand his trouble with addiction. I went down that path in my younger days and, same as him, came very close to death because of it. Thankfully, he had been doing amazingly well. He found work right away and helped us with doing things like cutting the grass, sweeping, and taking out the trash. He soon brought a girl named Simone up from Florida, and she moved in with us also. I didn't agree with it, but Steve was trying to let him do what he thought would make him happy and encourage him to get settled on his own.

"My honey!" Usually, he's in his easy chair watching TV when I get home from work. I would carefully straddle him in his big chair to give him a hug and a kiss, but today he was in the kitchen. I kicked my shoes off at the door and went straight to the bathroom to wash my hands.

With COVID going around these days, we had been taking every precaution, wearing masks, washing our hands more, taking shoes off inside the door, and even spraying down the groceries.

"My Pookie! Dinner's almost ready." He always calls me that. At first, I thought it was weird, but now I adore it. It's different. He was in the kitchen pulling steaks out of a marinade bag with tongs to go on the grill. I love it when he cooks.

He was busy with dinner, so instead of hugging for a few moments like we normally did, I just enjoyed the moment of coming together after my long, tiring day at work.

I asked him, "How do you feel?"

"Not too good. My sinuses are acting up," he answered as he laid the steaks on a tray to take outside to the grill.

"I'm sick," I said. "You know with Ma and Pa being in their eighties, and Simone being pregnant, we need to get tested for COVID." Thinking he probably wouldn't want to do that, I added, "It's easy. We can go through the drive-through at the drugstore and get it done for free."

"I know," he answered. "We'll go now."

I definitely didn't feel like it, but I knew we had to.

I saw David had gotten the mail, and my pile was lying next to my spot on the couch. I got my plate and settled into my spot on the couch to start going through my mail.

David came bouncing down the three flights of stairs.

"Thanks for getting the mail, sweetie. How's Simone feeling?"

"Oh, she's fine. What's for dinner?" David asked as he peeked into the kitchen at the steaks left in the pan on the stove. He looked disappointed and turned to walk away.

I knew he wouldn't eat the steak, but I said it anyway. "You know, they're really good. Your dad is like the steak whisperer when he picks them out."

He politely said no thanks and made himself a box of mac and cheese. He was on a no-beef, "healthier lifestyle" now, and Simone had been helping him with that too.

On January 31, 2021, Steve and I both tested positive for COVID, and my first thought was, *This is just like being sick with the flu for a few days, and wow! Two weeks off from work, paid! And all the things I can get done at home while I'm off!*

"We have to stay away from Ma and Pa no matter what!" I said to Steve while we were riding home. The ride home was surreal, like a weird dream. I thought, *This could turn into a kind of dream-come-true stay-home vacation or a complete nightmare at any moment,* as I tried to analyze the situation.

"Yeah, that's not going to be easy," he answered. "You know how they are. They're always thinking up ways to get us over there."

He was right, but I liked that they wanted us around and liked our company. Pa was always baking or cooking up something delicious, and Ma always had an understanding, listening ear. They have been good friends to me ever since we moved to South Carolina to stay with them before getting our own place. I enjoyed our yard sale adventures and breakfast outings together, and all the other things we did, laughing about silly things all along the way. They've always been good to us, and I sure didn't want them to get sick.

I was really concerned for Steve, though, after hearing all the stories of how it hit people with breathing problems or diabetes the hardest. That was why I took so many precautions to try and keep us from getting it. He was on insulin shots twice a day and a myriad of other medicines for high blood pressure and so forth.

That Saturday night, huge flakes of snow fell outside our bedroom window.

"Look, honey! It's beautiful!" I was mesmerized by the size of the flakes and how quickly the heavy flakes plummeted to the ground. The ground wasn't cold enough for it to stick, but it snowed into the wee hours of the morning. Steve had been sick in bed all week and didn't answer or seem to care as he lay there, half asleep. He could barely get up to go to the bathroom. I was still hurting all over with muscle aches; I was woozy and stuffy.

Another day passed, and Steve was having trouble breathing. David wanted to call an ambulance because despite our urging him all week to let us take him to the hospital, Steve had refused.

Finally, on Sunday, February 7, two days before his birthday, Steve said, "Maybe you'd better take me." I didn't think to pack anything but just got him in the car as quickly as possible. By the time we arrived at the emergency entrance, he could barely make it inside and had to stop and sit halfway. Once inside, I sat with him while he struggled to answer questions and surrendered his wallet and keys to me. They made me leave him there sitting in that chair. They made me go out and sit in the car. I wasn't allowed to stay. I wasn't allowed to hold his hand or stroke his forehead and tell him everything was going to be all right. There was nothing I could do to help or change things. I was powerless. My faith told me to hang on, but my mind was telling me that I was going to be left on my own again. I was stunned. I couldn't even cry.

I sat there in the cold thinking about all the times I had been left before. When I was left with my grandparents and they never came back. When my mother dropped me off at the movies and never came back or left me on my own to take care of my brother. How I couldn't wake her up for weeks, or how she never came to pick me up from detention after school. My first husband left me for another woman, and some crazy unseen force messed up my second marriage… Well, everything was messed up now for sure.

I remembered the verse that says,

Be strong and courageous. Do not be afraid, for the Lord will never leave you or forsake you. (Deut. 31:6)

There was nothing to do but go home. The what-if scenarios bombarded my thoughts continually. *What if he doesn't make it? What if we can't pay the bills? What if I don't know what to do? What if I don't do the right thing?* The list went on and on, torturing my mind day and night.

No, I fought back at those thoughts, *he's going to get better and come home, and everything is going to be okay again!* I repeated the verse over and over, every time I thought I might lose Steve, **"By Jesus's wounds we were healed" (Isa. 53:5).**

He gave us His Word, and that's the truth! I told myself, time after time.

I felt absolutely exhausted from the virus and had to force myself to move or do anything at all.

David tested positive but didn't seem sick at all, and Simone never tested positive, thank God, for I was worried about how it might affect her unborn baby.

They took Steve to the fifth-floor ICU diagnosed with COVID pneumonia. I couldn't visit or talk to him. I could only talk to a nurse or doctor when I called daily to see how he was doing. His staff changed daily, so I was talking to someone different every time I called, someone who didn't know me or him, obviously. They were pausing to look up things on paperwork which they were totally unfamiliar with, and I found this to be terribly frustrating and downright scary. I wondered if they had time to give him any attention at all.

He received his first antibody treatment on his birthday, February 9, and his second treatment the day after. Dr. Payne said they tried remdesivir, but he had an allergic reaction to hydroxychloroquine.

"*Oh my god!* What reaction?" I asked. I couldn't seem to get a straight answer.

The very next day was when things began to get dicey. Someone called from the hospital and said, "If you want to see him, you need to come now. Also bring your son."

How did they know about David? I wondered. He didn't talk to me very much these days, but I supposed he had been calling the hospital to check on his dad as well. Simone never talked to me except when absolutely necessary. She stayed in the bedroom upstairs all the time and didn't go to work or involve herself with me whatsoever. This was a disappointment as I had grand illusions of us becoming friends when she came to live with us, but it turned out that I didn't really know her at all even though we had lived in the same house for months. Occasionally, I heard her upstairs cursing at David over the phone when they were fighting. I tried to accept her elusiveness and let her be, but it still hurt my feelings to think I was being avoided for no apparent reason.

I called up the stairs, "David!" He poked his head out. "They said if we want to see Steve, we have to come *now*."

"Okay, give me a minute," David answered.

I called Ma and Pa to let them know what was going on. David was ready almost immediately, and we headed for the hospital.

I tried to stay calm as we drove forty-five minutes across town.

They gave us white coverings for our clothes and instructions about how to put them on so as not to contaminate them. They gave us face shields and hair covering. We looked like we were going into some kind of nuclear facility, but I was just thankful that I was finally going to get to see my husband after a week of sleepless nights and endless scenarios going around and around in my mind.

He lay there with his eyes closed, and I held his hand and kept saying, "Just rest and get better. Just rest and get better…"

David started crying at the foot of the bed and pleaded, "Daddy, please get well! We need you!" Then he hurriedly left the room.

Steve grasped my hand and opened his eyes long enough to say to me with a pleading look, "I'm sorry. I feel like I've let you down."

I wasn't sure how I kept from crying at that moment, but I felt I had to be strong and answered calmly, "You didn't let me down. Everything is going to be okay. Just rest and get better."

Then they told us we needed to go.

I tried to reassure David on the ride home, but I was scared stiff. They were moving Steve to a ventilator five days after being admitted to the hospital, which seemed to be a very bad sign indeed. The mortality rate, according to studies done, was usually slim for people after being placed on a ventilator. For people in his previous condition of health, about 3 percent survived.

When we arrived home, I got down on my face on my bedroom carpet and prayed the same prayer as I had so many years ago when I feared I would lose my son, Sarantis, before he was born.

For He has come to give us life and life abundantly. (John 10:10)

I know God's promises never change. This time, I prayed just as I had over twenty years ago for my unborn baby, "Lord, I know we don't aways get what we want, but I'm asking You to please bring my honey home to me. But no matter what, I'll trust You, for I know You love us more than we can ever imagine. Thank You, Father." That was when the tears began to flow and the reality of what might happen began to really set in. I know that God can do anything, but what He would actually do was still a mystery. I lay there and cried until I could cry no more. Then I began to try and figure out what I should do next.

First of all, I embarked on my almost daily task of texting about thirty friends, family, and work contacts to keep them up to date about what was happening, as well as contacting the insurance company that was handling Steve's short-term disability. The next question was how to figure out the bills.

"I need to talk with you, David." He walked out on the back deck with me. The evening was cool as we leaned on the deck rail and gazed across the lake. "I'm going to need your help with the bills until Steve gets out of the hospital. It's just temporary. If you could just pay half of the basic bills for a few weeks, then I can handle the rest." I showed him the figures I had come up with.

"Sure, Joye. I can do that," he answered without hesitation. I was more relieved than he'll ever know.

"Really, you don't know how much I appreciate that, David." We hugged and then went back to look out across the lake. The trees on the opposite shore caught my eye. The top of the tree line was an exact outline of Steve's profile lying down. "Look at the trees, David! It looks just like your dad! See his face…his nose and chin…

his hands folded on his chest." I traced the image through the air with my finger.

"Oh wow, that's crazy! It really does!" David marveled when he saw it.

Tears welled up as I thought, *We're with you, my honey, in our hearts. Just hang in there! We're right there with you!*

The next day, I went to the bank to get coin wrappers and transferred everything in savings over to checking. David and I spent several days figuring out how to get into the autopay bills on Steve's computer to figure out and make a list of what was due, and what was owed and when, and make sure everything was covered. We made phone calls and inquiries strategically going down the list, and finally David postponed my flight that Steve had booked for me before he got sick to go see the kids in Florida. My oldest daughter, Ria, graciously offered to come up to help me, but I didn't want to put a strain on her and her family and told her that we were handling things for now. I rolled every coin I could find to roll in the house and spent much of my time in front of the TV stripping wire that had been stored in the shed to take to the recycle place. I stopped eating out and began excavating the chest freezer. People from work gave us cards with money. Steve's nephew, TJ, brought food to the house. My eighty-year-old Aunt Martha sent five hundred dollars to help out. Every time a thought came to me that we wouldn't be able to make it financially, I quoted,

My God will meet all our needs according to the riches of His glory in Christ Jesus. (Phil. 4:19)

My days and nights were saturated in prayer and standing on His Word. Miraculously, we ended up with more than we had ever seen in our bank account before: nine thousand dollars!

Valentine's Day hit me especially hard. I asked the nurse on the phone what I could do. She told me that it was fine if I wanted to bring cards or flowers.

I looked at all the giant cards that Steve had given me over the years, and nothing I could do seemed to measure up. I carefully cut the faces of the cards apart and put them all together to make a gigantic banner with the message in big letters, "Love Always, Your Pookie!" I rolled it up and put it in the car. I stopped by Walmart and bought every rose I could find and took them to the hospital. I sat there feeling like a little kid, waiting on the bench for the nurse to come down.

A family of five, just outside the automatic doors, were huddled together crying over a family member that had just passed away. Every time the doors opened, I heard their mournful sobs. It was heartbreaking. It made everything seem like this was a pivotal time in my life as well, and the flood of emotion took my mind back to that dark place of fear and abandonment again.

The bench at the hospital was getting uncomfortable, and I wondered why it was taking so long for someone to come.

I pictured in my mind the disgust on some overworked nurse's face, and wondered what she would say, receiving a pain in the ass like me bringing them this mass of posterboard to hang and huge bunch of flowers to carry down long hallways to who-knows-where.

To my surprise, a sprightly little lady with a lovely face dressed in white scrubs and Crocs came to greet me. She was very friendly and assured me they would take care of everything. She also brought me his personal things in a bag and wondered if I had his wallet. I was relieved as it seemed that, after all, there really were people who cared and were taking care of my husband.

CHAPTER 9

Paradise Lost, Paradise Found

I felt guilty for even entertaining thoughts of what I'd do if Steve didn't pull through this. Emotions were running high. I needed someone to talk to, and I didn't want to upset and worry the kids any more than I already had. Ria had even offered to get off work and come up to help, but now I realized that I might really need her to come later on. Leaving the hospital, I drove straight to Ma and Pa's house. They were my mentors, and I needed a strong shoulder right about now.

Pa greeted me at the door. "Come on in and sit down," he said, ushering me to the kitchen table.

"I just came from the hospital," I said.

"We know. We just talked to David," Pa said, sitting at his usual place at the table. He looked worried, gazing down at the floor.

"There's some green tea in the cabinet." Ma pointed from her seat at the table. Her word puzzles were pushed to the side. "I know how you like that, so we got some just for you. Help yourself."

They weren't their usual calm, jovial selves. They were anxious and on edge, as was I. I told them about going to take the cards and flowers for Steve.

"I don't know what I would do without him," I told them, somehow without crying.

"Well, first of all, you don't need two cars," Pa said abruptly in his commanding tone. "You need to sell your car since it's in your name and keep his car to drive. That will save you some money."

My heart leapt in my chest. *Sell my car?*

Then Ma added, "You could turn the house over to David and Simone and stay in our spare bedroom. They could use the extra room with the baby coming."

My head was spinning, but I kept my cool. I figured they were just trying to help think of ways to take the burden of responsibility from me. I answered calmly, "No, I don't want to make any rash decisions right now." I ignored my angry feelings about possibly giving up, for the time being, and I drank my tea. We talked for a while, and then I left to go home.

David was acting strange. He was overenunciating and super fidgety.

I wondered if he had resorted to doing drugs again, under all the pressure lately. "David, you okay?"

"I'm fine. I'm just really tired. Why?" he asked.

"I don't know, you're not acting like yourself. You're not doing anything stupid, I hope." I tried to use a loving tone to remind him that I do sincerely care. We had gone together to Celebrate Recovery for some time, and I didn't want the worry of his dad to get him offtrack.

He understood what I meant. "I swear, I'm not doing anything! I'm *clean*, Joye!" He was adamant. "I'm just really tired." His voice was raspy.

There wasn't much more I could say at this point. "Okay. You know I love you, David." I put my hand on his arm.

"I love you too," he answered, and disappeared upstairs.

After they tried the first and second antibody treatment, Steve was put on the ventilator for eleven days. Since I had gone to visit him before they put him on the ventilator, I had to go back into quarantine for an additional week after having already taken my two weeks off paid from work. That took up all my vacation time.

He finally came off the ventilator on February 21, and they moved him to another room. I texted or called all our family, friends, and work. We rejoiced! This was a great sign! I would say, a miracle!

I still wasn't able to go see him until they moved him to a rehab facility. I had just started back to work that previous Monday and anxiously awaited the word from rehab about when I could come. March 2, I got the call and left work immediately to go visit him.

A long, curved, beautifully landscaped driveway led to an expansive building of stone and timber frame as I pulled up to park in front. I could hardly get inside fast enough to see my honey. I signed the clipboard and headed straight for his room.

Steve had a beard now. He lay in bed and just turned his eyes to meet mine. He had lost sixty-four pounds and was so weak that he could barely lift his head or move.

I sat on the edge of the bed and laid my head on his chest. "It's so good to see you!" The tears came now like a silent flood, and I just lay there thanking God that he had come back to me.

He seemed like he wasn't his old self anymore, though. Like his brain was in a fog and still trying to wake up. There was so much I wanted to tell him, but I had to give it some time.

I went to see him straight after work every day. A week after he had been in rehab, he still could barely lift his head. He got a call from David, and I helped Steve with his phone. He propped it to his ear, and I went to sit back in the chair. Then I could hear David's voice yelling on the phone from across the room. Steve wasn't saying anything.

This upset me. *What in the world could he be yelling at his dad about, especially when he's still trying to recover?* When they hung up, I asked, "What was all that about?"

"He's going to get garbage pickup instead of you taking the recycling," Steve answered quietly.

I was furious. "Oh no, no, he's not!"

Surprisingly, Steve sided with David and said he thought we should get trash pickup. This scared me, as I thought something had really happened to Steve's ability to reason. He knew how much it means to me to recycle. I know that sounds a little weird, but I feel very strongly about saving the earth, and recycling is one small way that I can contribute to that cause. I had even written and illustrated a children's book, yet to be published, called "Iguana's Garden" about a greedy iguana that indirectly teaches a little boy about recycling. Had Steve forgotten all these things about who I am? I didn't want to be lazy and get garbage pickup!

I vented, "It's *my* damn trash, and *I'm* not getting trash pickup! Nobody ever asked *me*, though!"

Poor Steve just lay there. He didn't have the strength to agree or disagree with anyone. I wondered, *Why is David acting like this? I don't make him take the trash to the recycling place. It's true that I do ask them to break down their food boxes, which I didn't think was that big of a deal.*

"Well, I don't know what's going on, but I'm heading home now to find out." I left earlier than usual, kissed Steve goodbye, and headed out the door.

When I got home, there were three full black garbage bags sitting inside the front door. *Well, that explains it*, I thought. *They must've cleaned out their room to get things ready for the baby.* I needed to take the trash anyway, so I loaded up the car. When I picked up their garbage bags, they were really heavy. *What's in here?* I wondered. *Maybe kitty litter.* I loaded them into the car.

When I got to the dump, I threw one of the garbage bags into the garbage dumpster below, but then curiosity got the best of me, and I wrestled to get the knot untied on the second bag. Looking inside, I couldn't believe my eyes… All the groceries from our pantry were in there!

I was so angry that the world just seemed to stop at that moment. My ears were ringing, and my head was pounding as I loaded the two remaining bags back into the car and drove home. I put the groceries back into the pantry at home.

I kept quiet and kept to myself all that evening. I tried to process what was happening so I could handle things the right way, but I couldn't make any sense of it. I couldn't sleep and just kept praying.

The next day, I got home from work and the outlet that hadn't been working on the kitchen wall was hanging out like a gutted fish.

The two of them were sitting on the floor pulling out all of my plastic containers from the corner cabinet. This was the first time I had seen Simone out of the bedroom and doing something in another part of the house since she had come to stay, four months ago.

"This is a mess under here!" David said. "You don't mind if we clean it out, do you?"

"Well, at least you're *asking*," I said coolly. I walked outside to the backyard before I could open my mouth and shoot back with something ugly.

I don't know if I ever would have had enough time to calm down enough to sit down and talk rationally with them, but when David came out on the back deck and started arguing with me because I wanted to hire someone to fix the kitchen outlet, I lost it. He lost it. Simone lost it. They ended up moving to their grandparents' house that day. *Oh great*, I thought. *Now Ma and Pa will be mad at me. The rest of the family might be mad at me. And, worst of all, Steve might be mad at me too.*

Thankfully, no one was mad at me. When Steve's brother, Slugger, asked what happened, I just said that David and I didn't see eye to eye. Slugger jokingly answered that it was because David was taller than me.

Steve came home from rehab a week later to his single bed set up in the middle of the living room. It was still too hard for him to make it up the stairs. I took care of his personal needs in the morning before I went to work, and Ma and Pa came over every single day to sit with him and keep him company. It did him a lot of good, I think, that they did that, even though he wouldn't admit it. I think it did them some good to be able to help too.

A couple of weeks went by, and David called his dad to ask if he could come over and borrow something. I was afraid we would get into another fight.

He was getting ready to leave and said, "I love you guys," over his shoulder.

He said "you guys"! That means both of us, I thought.

I seized my opportunity and called to him, "David, wait!"

He stopped, and I asked him, "Can I have a hug?"

He gave me a warm hug, and I said, "I'm so sorry about what happened. I'm sorry I lost my temper."

"We all lost our temper. I'm sorry too," he said.

After they got into their own place, I got the chance to talk to Simone also, although as much as I wanted to, I never asked for an explanation from either of them.

One morning as I lay in bed, halfway between awake and asleep, a voice spoke to me and said, "Forgiveness is like a warm blanket on a cold night."

* * * * *

During this time, I met my good friend April at work. We hit it off immediately, but our lead didn't like for us to talk while we were working, so we wrote notes to each other. We had an unusual connection by the Holy Spirit. We were both having husband issues at that time.

I looked to see if anyone was watching. "April!" I called to her just above a whisper to get her attention. Through the clear plastic that they had installed between all the stations for COVID, I showed her my scripture for the day that I had written to memorize on a three-by-five-inch index card.

Rejoice! Do not be anxious about anything, but in everything, by prayer and petition, with thanksgiving, present your requests to God. (Phil. 4:6)

"I'm not going to let anything get the best of me today!" I added.

April sat up tall and straight at her station next to mine. She is a beautiful Black woman with an electric personality I was immediately drawn to. She tossed her curls excitedly and showed me her devotional, *Jesus Calling* by Sarah Young, which she called her "Daily Bread." That was the verse for that day, May 11! She showed me her yellow sticky note through the clear plastic barrier. It read, "Stay Fluffy!!!" Then she made a spraying gesture like she was spraying herself down with PAM, as she would say. We both laughed and went back to our soldering.

Many times, our prayers and scriptures lined up. We prayed for each other, and I bought a copy of her beloved devotional, which has been a huge blessing to me ever since. I believe God was preparing me through April for another season of growing spiritually, which is often painful and rarely easy.

We soon became close friends, but a turn of events had me end up in another area of the plant called JDAM (joint direct attack munition), soldering cables on a fast-paced assembly line.

Leah was the lead over that area of over forty people in one big room at the back of the plant. She came out of the office, her voice booming over the chatter and rhythmic clanking of machinery. "JDAM, listen up! Our number has increased to 120 cables per day. We need to be working ten hours a day, Monday through Friday, eight hours on Saturday and possibly Sunday, depending on how many we get done. If we don't make our numbers, then it carries over to the next day and so on. Okay, guys, we got this!"

Despite her undying optimism, everyone hung their heads in desperation. Unfortunately, Leah's "talk" had the opposite effect on some people. This was bad because, if one person on the line decided they didn't want to work that hard, then it put everyone else behind too. We were all exhausted already.

The line was set up with each station working on a three-minute segment of the total operation to complete each cable. We switched stations after every break to alleviate repetitious movement contributing to carpal tunnel nerve damage. I worked in JDAM for over eight months, almost the whole year that Steve was at home recovering from COVID.

I sat down at the jumper station only to find that sticky flux was spilled everywhere, tools were missing, the floor was a mess, and I was out of solder. I took a deep breath and tried to keep my patience while I got up to go find a roll of solder, if there was any. The next station was already waiting for me to pass a cable.

Why am I working here, of all places? I questioned. *I feel like I've been kidnapped and sold into slavery for the basic necessities of life—*

food, clothing, a roof over my head, and transportation to get here. This is no life!

After I had sat quietly for some time and calmed down, the Lord spoke to my heart, *I am preparing you for days of prosperity and freedom.* I wrote this down in my little black four-by-six notebook that I always carry as I waited for my next cable.

Then I wondered to myself, **Love always protects (2 Cor. 13).** *Am I doing my part to protect my country by building cables for the military? Is that what the Lord meant by freedom? Or maybe preparing for retirement!* I liked the thought of retirement.

We were all later than the usual time of getting off at 3:30, so hitting the 5:00 p.m. traffic going home on the already long forty-five-minute commute turned into an hour and a half. I didn't get home until dark, and when I walked in, I saw that Ma and Pa had already gone home. Steve was waiting for me in his chair. It had been more than two months since Steve had come home, and he had just started getting around with a cane. While Steve was in the hospital, they hadn't moved his leg away from the bedrail, which had caused nerve damage in his foot. He was having a lot of pain still, but he could drive now. However, the diagnosis was permanent COPD, which made it hard for him to walk any distance without stopping for a rest. He had also torn a muscle in his arm from trying to lift himself out of bed. It seemed everything for him was a major struggle, yet he remained determined to get better, and was walking without the cane in just two weeks.

I was exhausted and aggravated from the long day. I plopped on the couch. "So what did you guys do today?" I tried to be as cheerful as possible.

"Oh, we went to lunch and did the shopping," he answered.

I felt jealous and angry that I had worked so hard all day while they ran around having a good time. I missed my outings with Steve and Ma and Pa. I never got to go with them anymore.

His bed in the middle of our living room needed the sheets changed. There were piles of pills, piles of boxes of things, piles of mail on the coffee table, clothes on top of clothes hanging on the hall tree. The grass needed to be cut, but I had to work all day Saturday. The list went on and on.

I was also worried about the bank account, which was steadily dwindling.

"*And* I did two laps around the track at rehab today!" he announced proudly. "They sent me another letter saying that I qualify for permanent disability, but I've made up my mind. I'm going back to work!"

Never realizing what a struggle rehabilitation was for him, all I could think of was how out of control everything was.

"Oh, that's great," I said half-heartedly, and thought, *But you couldn't put your dishes in the sink to help me.*

"Would you fix me some ramen noodles?" he asked meekly, knowing I was tired.

I didn't answer and just started banging things around in the kitchen. I cooked the noodles and slopped them into a bowl as fast as I could. I sat the bowl on his TV stand.

I glanced over to see his head hanging down, which made me feel guilty now, on top of everything else. And that made me even angrier. I stomped upstairs to the bedroom and sat on the edge of the bed to catch my breath. I started to cry uncontrollably.

"God, I can't do this anymore! Please help me!" I thought about running away, but that was out of the question because that would definitely only make me feel worse. I love Steve too much to do a crazy thing like that.

The next morning, while driving to work, I listened to Joyce Meyer talk about how she would get upset with her husband, Dave. She said, "The Lord spoke to me and said, 'Joyce, you're not going to be able to go to the next level of spiritual maturity until you treat your husband the right way.'"

The scriptures came to my mind,

Do everything without complaining or arguing, so that you may become blameless and pure, a child of God without fault. (Phil. 2:14)

And

Serve as unto the Lord, and not as unto men. (Col. 3:23)

And

Jesus said, "Whatever you've done for the least of these, you've done it unto Me." (Matt. 25:40)

"I'm so sorry, Lord." I cried all morning at work. I had been treating Steve terribly, and it wasn't even his fault.

The Lord spoke to my heart. *Focus on what you can do about your things right now, and let Me fix the rest in My way, in My time. Trust Me.*

Then there were the financial problems. I kept thinking about all the money we had when Steve first got sick, and now our bank account just kept shrinking, lower and lower.

October rolled around, and the big day finally came for Steve's doctor to evaluate whether or not he could return to work. The answer came back no, and he was devastated.

"I never missed my sessions! I worked so hard! We can't live on disability!" He was angry and then fell into a deep depression, just watching TV, hour after hour, day after day.

At the end of December, he refused permanent disability again and asked the doctor to please send him to work with restrictions. He was at work for three days in the first week of January before they sent him home to finish recovering and come back when there were no restrictions.

In the meantime, our lead, Leah, announced that we would be working on Sundays as well.

When she went into her office, I got up from the line and paced back and forth. I had to make a decision, here and now. I was ready to walk out. How could I leave my husband at home all these months like this? And was I trying to kill myself working seventy hours a week? Physically, it was just impossible for me to continue. I walked over to Cookie Mack's station. Cookie is a rock. She's tough, and she'll tell it like it is. She's the kind of woman you would want running things for you.

"Cookie! I can't do this!" I said in desperation.

She threw up her hands and said simply, "Give it to God! Just give it to God!"

Well, I had heard this phrase before, but now the understanding of it suddenly seemed to be clear to me.

That night when I got home, I went straight upstairs and got down on my face in prayer. "Lord, I give it all to You. My body, my time, my job, Steve, my home, my children, everything! I can't do this in my own strength, Lord! I need You!"

It was a few nights later, around twelve midnight, when I woke up with three words ringing in my head. They were so clear and persistent that I had to get up and write them down on one of my three-by-five cards to keep with me at all times: *He will SUSTAIN me, RENEW me, UPHOLD me.* He spoke to my heart to *stay in that word, and not complain,* even though I was constantly surrounded by complaining and had done my fair share. *Remember the Israelites! I am preparing you for days of abundance and freedom ahead.* I thought of the dream of Jesus and the martyrs I had when I was young, and how I didn't understand why He showed me such a strange vision at the time, but now I knew. True Christianity means total surrender, even unto death.

I prayed, "Lord, please help me surrender to You!"

A New To-Do List

- No criticizing, complaining, or blaming someone else for my problems. Rise above by faith.
- Only say things that are good about other people. Stay in forgiveness. Walk in love.
- Be brave, not lazy and disobedient. No excuses. Trust God.

When I walked through the door after work, I found Steve holding his head in his hands.

"What's the matter, sweetie?"

"There was a misunderstanding with the insurance company, and they've stopped my disability since January 1. They thought I would be starting back to work, but as you know, that didn't happen because work sent me home after three days." He was very upset with tears in his eyes.

If I said I wasn't upset, I'd be lying. I fussed and fumed, paced and cried. We went from having $9,000 in our bank account when Steve got sick to our current balance of $9.

I got on the phone and tried to straighten things out, only to get the runaround from insurance to doctor to people services because we had no physical HR at work, and back to the insurance company again.

There is a direct connection between obedience and prosperity, and disobedience and hardship. I had to stop murmuring and blathering, and start trusting and obeying.

The next morning, I awoke to praying over and over in my sleep, "Lord, please help me obey…help me obey You, Lord!"

I got a phone call from my niece telling me that Aunt Brenda had passed away from COVID.

It was a cold, gray day in the last dregs of winter as I took my usual walk during breaktime at work. As I rounded the corner at the front of the building, a bright blue flash caught my eye. I looked up into the lacey bare branches of the crepe myrtles and, just a few feet away, a northeastern bluebird met my gaze—a shock of sapphire against that dreary gray sky. I wondered what it could be doing here alone at this cold time of the year. My heart leapt as it took flight, and I knew. She had come to tell me that, like the happy little bluebird, it was time for me to fly.

Every time I thought about how we weren't going to make it, I refused to go by feelings or unbelief. I diligently studied God's principles every day and was prepared to pull out one of my index cards:

> **He holds victory in store for me, He is my shield, He guards my course, He protects His faithful ones. (Prov. 2:6–8)**

I trust You, Lord, and I am safe. I commit my way and trust in Him, and He makes my justice shine! I am still and wait for Him. I do not fret. I enjoy great peace! (Psa. 37:3–11)

You grant me relief from days of trouble. And when anxiety was great within me, Your consolation brought joy to my soul. (Psa. 94:13)

God is amazing. We received a check for five hundred dollars a couple of weeks later, not the full amount we were expecting but enough to get by. Then another check came on the twenty-third for $2,600. Ma and Pa helped us out, and then we received another check for the amount we were behind on for $4,300. We never had to spend what Ma and Pa loaned us. We were able to pay them back right away and make our bills on time.

While Steve was still in a wheelchair, Martha, Ria, Naia, Callie, and Mary came to visit. We met my Uncle Paul and my brother, Bryan, for a big family picnic at the park.

Then Martha paid for us to see the breathtaking gardens in late spring at the Biltmore House.

As I struggled trying to push Steve up the front parking lot at the Biltmore House, Ria noticed that I was having a hard time. "Mom, let me take a turn." She smiled and took over for me.

Then Mary came along just as we arrived at a steep incline. "I got this!" She relieved her sister and took off like a shot to the top of the hill.

Martha and I looked up to see Ria, Mary, and Steve at the top smiling proudly ear to ear, and I thought how far we've come as a family! My heart filled to overflowing with love as I thought about how two angry teenage girls have become beautiful, caring young women. How good it is to be loved!

Steve went back to work full-time in maintenance with no restrictions on May 3, 2022. Now his handicap card hangs from the rearview mirror of his dream car in the employee parking lot, a metallic midnight-blue Nissan 370 Z.

I have decided I like working on Saturdays now since I can use that money to give more, start saving up for a new driveway, and take trips to see the family, unless God has a better plan.

Spring had arrived, and since it was a busy day at work, after dinner I decided to go for a short walk. I stepped outside into the cool, late afternoon. It was just the right temperature. The yellow daffodils swayed their pretty heads, nodding in the breeze. The birds twittered through the treetops, and the squirrels skittered about, hunting something soft for their nests, preparing for the arrival of their young. The earth and the air smelled sweet and fresh.

As I headed up the road to the top of the hill, the golden sun filled the sky with the most beautiful shade of peachy gold I have ever seen. My heart filled with so much joy that I could hardly express it.

A new affirmation: "Lord, thank You for being here with me in this moment. All I need is You. So what will our next adventure be, Lord?"

What about that book you said you wanted to write?

The End...and the Beginning

A POEM

Bluebird Cottage

This poem's for you, as I have now learned
That this home wasn't mine to build or to earn.
It isn't a shelter from the world's wind and cold,
For storms that are weathered bring the wisdom of old.
The *Caretaker* bought *me*, this rough mountainside,
Because of His dream to bring His family a new life.
At the *heart* of the forest was a heap of cold stone,
Where I longed for, but couldn't, make a place to call home.
When I finally offered to let Him place every beam
He fashioned a cottage that satisfied my dream,
With music and laughter to soothe my weary soul,
Some sunlight and rain to make my faith grow.
It took Him my lifetime to pull out each thorny vine,
And replace it with honeysuckle, a fragrance divine.
Now His Spirit's a bluebird, humbly living inside,
Where we're happy and free, and love taught me to fly.
Where loved ones come to gather and share
In this message to all, everyone, everywhere:
My God is my shelter, the earth is my test.
To God be the glory, my peace, and my rest.

ABOUT THE AUTHOR

Joye Frost and her husband, Steven, live near his family in beautiful South Carolina in the foothills of the Great Smoky Mountains.

Learning God's principles of love and faith, and with his help, putting them into practice is the calling and focal point of her life. She has a degree in Christian family counseling along with an interest in sustainable living, recycling, and a great love of nature.

Joye attends LifeSong Church, a non-denominational Christian church in Lyman where she also enjoys a weekly Bible study with her friends. Some of her favorite pastimes include traveling to visit her grown children in Florida, writing, painting, and creating picture books for their seven grandchildren.